This ecumenical guide to the restored catechumenate
stories, sample outlines for instructional sessions, ev
merely to increase their membership, but to make di
ing the catechumenate as well as those already engag
assistance in this accessible handbook.
Gail Ramshaw, Professor of Religion, La Salle University, Philadelphia

The practices commended in this fully ecumenical handbook on the catechumenate provide ancient-future wisdom at its best. Such practices invite congregations to move baptism and its attendant formational disciplines to the very center of church life and mission. *Go Make Disciples* gives detailed and flexible ways for congregations to walk this baptismal way.
Mark W. Stamm, Associate Professor of Christian Worship, Perkins School of Theology,
Southern Methodist University, Dallas

This is the handbook I wish had been available fifteen years ago when beginning the process in the congregation. It will give this wonderful, ancient/future practice of the catechumenate wings to take off from its theoretical and historical base.
Britt Olson, Canon to the Ordinary, Northern California Episcopal Diocese

I read *Go Make Disciples* and I wanted to buy it and share it with my team today! This is the most helpful, practical, and comprehensive resource for welcoming seekers and forming disciples currently available.
Daniel Benedict, abbot of the Order of Saint Luke and a presbyter in The United Methodist Church

Congregations across North America are experiencing renewal as they welcome adult newcomers to the lifelong, life-giving, and life-changing depths of Christian baptism. In this book a roundtable of expert practitioners and thinkers share their own experience and resources across the boundaries of liturgical cultures and denominations.
Benjamin M. Stewart, Assistant Professor of Worship and Dean of Augustana Chapel,
Lutheran School of Theology at Chicago

Our cultural change is intense for pastoral ministry, and because of it a wave of attention has turned from the management of church as institution to the recognition of the church as agent in mission. But this very change leads to new thoughts and perspective on baptism itself; in other words, how is baptism more than just a cultural hold-over from Christendom, and rather a life-giving practice of disciple making? *Go Makes Disciples* offers the church an incredibly helpful handbook to explore these important issues.
Andrew Root, Associate Professor of Youth and Family Ministry at Luther Seminary, St. Paul

Recovering Christian initiation as a part of a congregation's mission always brings new life into the congregation. Now those congregations that want to recover this exciting part of mission have a handbook to help them begin!
Timothy W. Whitaker, Florida Area Resident Bishop, The United Methodist Church

There is much talk today about declining church membership. *Go Make Disciples* offers a refreshing and very practical contribution to this conversation by returning the focus to discipleship through baptism and the nurturing of faith through the process of the catechumenate. This handbook is a timely resource, valuable to any Christian community of faith.
Peter J. L. Perella, Director for Worship Formation and Liturgical Resources,
Evangelical Lutheran Church in America

This resource is a long-awaited guide for congregations entering into this dynamic process of adult formation. Well-organized materials include step-by-step guides, checklists, prayers, liturgical resources, and session plans. The process is meant to be extravagant with time, welcome, prayer, formation, support, and spirituality. The authors encourage flexibility and adaptation to meet the unique capacities of the congregation and needs of the seekers. *Go Make Disciples* is important for all congregations embarking on a journey into a transformational ministry through the waters of baptism.

Ann McElligott, Episcopal priest

If it is true that "Christians are made, not born," this book will be a treasure trove for Christian communities who are serious about accompanying adult seekers to the waters of baptism and energizing the life of those already baptized. *Go Make Disciples* is a game changer for the way we do church. Something new and something old: not another program, but an invitation to a journey of formation with Christ and the church.

Robert G. Schaefer, lead pastor, Emmanuel Lutheran Church, Venice, Florida

This ecumenical team of collaborators is to be commended for giving the greater church such a concise and thorough handbook on the reclaimed catechumenal process. Advocates who already enthusiastically endorse this process will appreciate the refresher points and all who want to grow the kingdom of God will experience how to "live wet."

Clifford King Harbin, catechumenal process local leader and national trainer of teams since 1990 in the Episcopal and United Methodist traditions

Go Make Disciples is the resource I've been longing for. Welcoming newcomers and forming disciples is what healthy congregations do. This deeply constructive resource invites congregations to take up those two central tasks together in faith. "We have a way, come and see!"

Jessicah Krey Duckworth, Assistant Professor of Congregational and Community Care Leadership, Luther Seminary, St. Paul

This is the perfect resource to move the ancient catechumenal process of disciple making into the mainstream of North American Christian faith communities. Presented in bite-sized pieces that are informative without being academic or simplistic, everything needed to begin and practice the catechumenate is in your hands.

Sherman Hesselgrave, Incumbent, Church of the Holy Trinity, Toronto

The retrieval of the ancient church's pattern of Christian initiation and formation is a significant element of the response to our post-Christendom context. Experience shows that every congregation, as it seeks to make disciples, will have its own unique capacity to respond to the needs of this context. This handbook, created by a team with tremendous knowledge and experience in this area, is designed to serve the interests of Christian communities across a broad spectrum of potential. For many years, I think, it will be a standard and necessary reference for congregations in missional transition.

Mark MacDonald, National Indigenous Anglican Bishop, Anglican Church of Canada

In the quest to cultivate vital and faithful congregations for the twenty-first century, today's need is a renewed way of being church, one that contours lives in the path of discipleship. This volume is a "must have" companion in that work, offering well-grounded rationale, compelling real life stories and practical how-to advice for fostering robust baptismal living by your community of faith.

Jay Koyle, President, the Associated Parishes for Liturgy and Mission

Go Make Disciples

An Invitation to
Baptismal Living

A Handbook to the Catechumenate

AUGSBURG FORTRESS

GO MAKE DISCIPLES: AN INVITATION TO BAPTISMAL LIVING
A Handbook to the Catechumenate

Also available:
Go Make Disciples Companion CD-ROM (ISBN 978-1-4514-2613-7)
Welcome, Child of God (ISBN 978-1-4514-0133-2); a board book for infants and toddlers
Washed and Welcome: A Baptism Sourcebook (ISBN 978-1-4514-0130-1)
Living the Promises of Baptism: 101 Ideas for Parents (ISBN 978-1-4514-0131-8)

Unless otherwise indicated, scripture quotations are from the New Revised Standard Version Bible © 1989 Division of Christian Education of the National Council of the Churches of Christ in the United States of America. Used by permission. All rights reserved.

Editors: Dennis Bushkofsky, Suzanne Burke, and Richard Rouse
Cover illustration: Claudia McGehee
Interior art: Claudia McGehee
Cover and interior design: Ivy Palmer Skrade

ISBN 978-1-4514-2612-0

Printed in the U.S.A.

18 17 16 15 14 13 12   2 3 4 5 6 7

This life, therefore, is not godliness
but the process of becoming godly,
not health but getting well,
not being but becoming,
not rest but exercise.
We are not now what we shall be,
but we are on the way.
The process is not yet finished,
but it is actively going on.
This is not the goal but it is the right road.
At present, everything does not gleam and sparkle,
but everything is being cleansed.

–Martin Luther

Contents

Exploration

Intense Preparation

Baptismal Living

Additional Resources

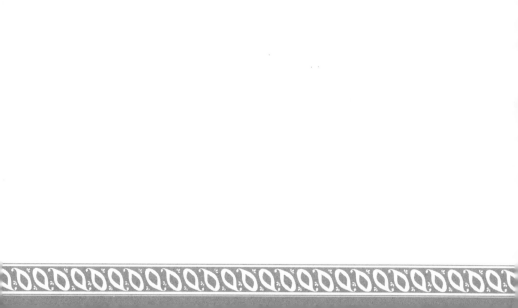

Foreword

I remember hot summers as a kid in an era when most families didn't have air conditioning in their homes. We would hang out for hours at the community pool. We would visit the nearest body of water, be it a lake or the ocean. And if we were lucky, our parents might take us to a water park where we would spend the day walking wet as we enjoyed rafting on the lazy river ride or cascading through numerous colored tubes that came splashing down into a cool pool of water. There was a sign at one such park that advertised: "Water is life. Live it large."

Water. Refreshing. Renewing. Life-giving. We think of the water of baptism that is all these things and more. As water is poured over the head of a child or adult, or one is immersed in a baptismal pool, the miracle of new life in Christ begins to transform us. The ancient church made new disciples while preparing them for baptism and conversion to a new way of living in a process known as the *catechumenate*. The catechumenate has been reclaimed for that same purpose in our own time in order to help people become disciples of Jesus Christ. The catechumenal process also enables people to be more fully conscious of baptism's impact in their daily lives. That's what it means to walk wet: to remember and live out baptism each day as disciples of Jesus in today's world.

The goal in this volume is to provide a handbook for pastors, catechists, evangelism teams, and other congregational leaders that is accessible, fun, and grace-filled, to help you introduce and implement the incredible gift of baptism more fully into the life and ministry of your faith community. To our knowledge this is the first fully ecumenical handbook based on the catechumenate, with eighteen contributors and practitioners from various mainline Christian denominations involved in the project. It is a resource that can be used by any size congregation. And while the disciple making process outlined in this book is common to many denominations, there are worship rites and practices that are distinctly different from one denomination to another. Many specific denominational resources, as well as other items intended for group use and distribution, are available on a companion CD-ROM ❂ (a separate purchase), and will supplement the primary materials published in this handbook.

Walk wet and enjoy the journey!

–Rick Rouse, president, North American Association for the Catechumenate

Introduction

Welcome to Making Disciples!

Go Make Disciples is not fundamentally about increasing numbers, making new members, or receiving a bigger weekly offering, but about *discipleship*. This is the first and foremost goal to keep in mind about this book. In our day, when worship has expanded out of traditional forms and spaces into many new styles and considerable diversity in order to attract as many people as possible, we are reminded of a startling reality: since the early centuries of the Christian church seekers were invited into the way of Jesus Christ through intentional instruction about the life of faith and the symbols and rituals that could sustain them in a community. It was known as a *catechumenate*.

We might then think about this handbook as providing some guidance into ways that a Christian community might work with seekers today. To those who are looking for a deeper meaning to life, a faith community says, Come and see what we do! Making disciples is about living and sharing the faith through symbols, rituals, and story with those who have either become distanced from a local community of faith or have never really encountered one. It is the first step where we share a story; not just any story, but a story about Jesus. We share that story not just verbally, but through the ways that we live and worship together. Jesus—the incarnate Word of God—literally takes flesh in a congregation of Christian believers. The congregation then offers seekers a way to take part in a story that is often very different from those presented by various contemporary media outlets.

This handbook is for those of us who wish to find help in proclaiming the gospel of Jesus Christ through instruction, worship, symbols, and art to people we encounter in our communities. You may be in a congregation that has recently struggled with finding its voice in an established—even ostensibly Christian—neighborhood. Yet all of a sudden you realize that you and others in your congregation don't even know the gospel story that well yourself. It may have been many years since you were in a confirmation class. You may have set out on a path of spiritual renewal within your congregation and have found that you have a story to share in words and deeds with neighbors around you, possibly even with neighbors who never took notice of your congregation in their midst. Perhaps now you are wondering how to invite others into a life of following Jesus Christ.

Or maybe you are in a community where a majority of people have no religious affiliation or history (sometimes called the *none* segment by sociologists). As with many communities of faith in the earliest centuries of the Christian church, you may be a part of a congregation that in its own intensity and seriousness draws people toward your worship and service to the neighborhood and to the world beyond. You begin catechetical instruction from the very beginning, that is, simply telling the story of Jesus and inviting people into the rich fare that the community of faith offers. And you give these seekers a language: symbols and rituals that can sustain and to which people can cling especially when the going gets rough (and we all know the many bumps life offers us).

These are but two examples, and this handbook is definitely not limited to them. This handbook is intended for all congregations seeking to welcome others into the Christian faith. This handbook is also about helping you as a catechist, pastor, worship leader, musician, educator, sponsor, or other leader in the joyful task of forming other disciples in the body of Christ. Ultimately this handbook is for everyone who has questions about how to live out God's call to baptism and beyond. These questions might range from the simple to the complex. This handbook is for those who wish to respond with generosity to unchurched or uncatechized parents bringing their children for baptism. This handbook is for those who wish they had a clearer approach to the practice of baptism in their congregation. This handbook is for those wishing to deepen the life of faith in their community and for those wishing to live the Christian faith consciously as a form of invitation for all of their diverse neighbors. This handbook is for inviting unbaptized people into faith and for encouraging already baptized people to live out their faith more fully. This handbook is for you!

Using This Handbook

Many of us may remember learning how to swim. It can be both scary and exhilarating. For those congregations just starting the process of intentionally making disciples, it may likewise be daunting and exciting at the same time. That's why we have designed this handbook to help you get started, from taking those first simple strokes to moving confidently through the deeper waters of guiding people on a faith journey.

One public swimming pool advertised during a hot summer: come live in the water! And that is precisely the invitation for making disciples, to enter into a process that includes immersion in the waters of baptism and then continues as one draws from the wellspring of faith in Jesus Christ. This handbook is intended to help congregations implement the task of making disciples in their own community.

The remaining part of the **Introduction** is intended to help leaders of a congregation's disciple making ministry understand some significant shifts taking place in the religious landscape, particularly in North America. While becoming a Christian has always meant learning to follow Jesus Christ, for centuries this was often represented more in institutional terms: becoming a member of the church. As many younger generations of people these days often belong to fewer face-to-face formal organizations and associations, it may be more helpful—and in many ways more accurate—to consider the importance of *discipleship* rather than membership. The remainder of the Introduction describes a four-fold shape of guiding people to baptism and beyond that many people understand today as a *catechumenate*.

Getting Started offers congregational leaders a rationale for using the disciple making process described in this book, as well as providing ways to determine how ready your congregation might be to use this process. The chapter concludes with a number of practical guidelines to use in setting up disciple making teams, recruiting leaders and sponsors, and providing a launch guide and checklist as you get started with a disciple making process in your own congregation.

In many ways the four chapters that follow are the heart of this handbook, since they provide details about the stages of the four-fold shape of accompanying candidates to baptism or affirmation of baptism and beyond. Quite likely the chapters on **Inquiry** (pages 75-92), **Exploration** (pages 93-106), **Intense Preparation** (pages 107-123), and **Baptismal Living** (pages 125-137) will be used over and over again by congregational leaders who are involved in the task of making disciples. This handbook provides a handy icon tab at the right edge of each page in the chapters detailing the specific tasks in the four-fold shape of disciple making. Since many of this book's resources are specific to certain points of a process, no doubt users will find these visual cues and organizational methods helpful.

Because congregations will be involved in disciple making with those who have not yet been baptized, as well as working with people who have already been baptized, this handbook distinguishes between those two designations in a variety of ways. During occasions of congregational worship when participants in the discipleship process are welcomed and supported by prayers and various actions, those who are preparing for baptism will be acknowledged in different ways from participants who have already been baptized. While unbaptized and baptized participants in a disciple making process may join together for many instructional sessions, if there are both types of candidates it will likely be helpful to have different small groups that make this distinction, so that unbaptized participants may be supported in one way and baptized participants in another way.

This handbook concludes with a large chapter of **Additional Resources** (pages 139-206), providing a number of materials that will help readers to understand the process of making disciples in greater depth. Many contributions by actual users of this process help congregations with scripture reflection methods, session designs, prayers, and blessings to use in disciple making groups. A number of denominations have produced worship resources and other materials for welcoming and accompanying new disciples, and these are described at some length in the concluding chapter. Several pages demonstrate how to make important connections between a process of making disciples and a congregation's ongoing worship life. Two separate resources describe the history and mission of the catechumenate in some detail. A glossary will prove to be handy for many people, since there are a number of specific terms that describe the process and relationships involved in making disciples. A bibliography of additional resources will guide people to just some of the vast array of materials that exist beyond this book. Finally, a list of the contents of materials on the **companion CD-ROM*** to this handbook will help leaders know what other materials are readily available in PDF or customizable RTF format for group distribution.

*When a resource mentioned in this handbook is available on the companion CD-ROM, a ❁ symbol indicates this.

The Shift from Membership to Discipleship

Recent decades have witnessed a decline in mainline Christian denominations. National polls reveal that the percentage of people in North America who identify themselves as Christian has slipped, and that a growing number of individuals respond *none* when asked about their religious affiliation. For many, this represents a waning influence of the Christian church on the larger and increasingly secular North American culture. Scholars often suggest that we have entered into a *post-Christian* era.

At the same time, congregations are rediscovering what it means to be a church in mission and to build connections with a large number of unchurched people at or near their front doors. These congregations acknowledge that the great commission of Jesus is at the heart of the church's mission: "Go . . . make disciples of all nations, baptizing them in the name of the Father and of the Son and of the Holy Spirit" (Matt. 28:19). For the Christian church to survive as well as thrive, it must in some ways return to the example of the early church in the New Testament.

In their book, *A Field Guide for the Missional Congregation*, Rick Rouse and Craig Van Gelder write:

> The missional church is not about maintenance or survival as an institution, but rather about participating more fully in God's mission. It is not focused so much on the number of members, but rather on how well people are living out their faith in daily discipleship. Its ministry is not so much centered on the work of the pastor, but rather on empowering the laity (non-clergy) for their ministry in daily life. While a chaplaincy church may view caring for its members as an end in itself, a missional congregation will provide care as a *means to an end*—to help its disciples be healthy and effective in their efforts to reach out to others with the love of God in Christ.
>
> This requires a paradigm shift from maintenance to mission, from membership to discipleship. As congregations take seriously the task of making disciples, many are reclaiming this ancient-future gift of the church known as the catechumenate—with its focus on faith formation, disciple-making, and baptismal living. The disciple making process invites people into a deeper faith journey that is intended to lead to transformation and a new way of life as modern day disciples of Jesus.

Consider the following example from a faith community we'll call Alleluia Church.

MORE THAN MEMBERSHIP 🌐

We are glad you are a part of the Alleluia Church community! We are about reaching people with God's unconditional acceptance and grace in Jesus Christ to make lives whole. We pray that you have been touched by God's grace during your time here. We invite you to deepen your relationship with God by joining our disciple making process, during which you can continue to experience God's love and grow in your faith.

God's dream for Alleluia Church is our vision—bringing healing and wholeness to lives and all creation. Our mission is to live out Jesus' invitation to come and see, come and grow, come and serve.

To live out our mission and vision, we offer a disciple making process as a gift to all those new to our community. Although you will become a member of Alleluia as a part of this process, the focus of this process is not on membership, but on helping you grow in discipleship. We recognize a life of faith is not about being a member but about being a follower of Christ in a community of believers.

We invite you to learn more about this process by attending our inquiry sessions. If you decide this disciple making process is not for you at this time, you have other options, which include meeting privately with a faith mentor, transferring your membership to Alleluia, or going through the disciple making process at a later time.

This chart [on the following page] will help you understand our approach at Alleluia Church as we focus on a way of discipleship that goes beyond simple church membership.

WAY OF MEMBERSHIP	WAY OF DISCIPLESHIP
New member classes	Disciple making process
New people conform to the way we do things	New people transform congregation and even challenge how we do things
We give you the answers	You raise the questions
Voting member only needs to commune once and make a contribution of record each year	Discipleship is a way of life
Church provides you with all you need to be Christian (in an hour a week!)	Living as a Christian is a 24/7 proposition, that mostly happens away from church
Get it done!	Live it out!
Focus on destination: becoming a member	Focus on the journey: walking as a disciple
Disseminating information	Building relationships with God, self, and others
Assenting to doctrine	Practicing faith through prayer, Bible reading, worship, and ministry in daily life
Limited time span	As long as it takes
For new members only	For the whole congregation through serving as faith partners and blessings in worship
Pastor-driven	Lay-driven
New member orientation	Faith formation

Shifting to Discipleship: Stories from the Field

As you page through the resources of this book you will catch glimpses of what can happen when congregations place renewed emphasis on Christ's commission to make disciples. Christian discipleship is a way of life, one that involves the nurture of relationships and reorientation to life as citizens of the promised reign of God. Because of its focus on formation for baptismal living, the ancient catechumenate is being adapted for today with amazing results.

This seems like a development of significant potential and it actually is. Be aware that scenes sketched on the printed page can appear more tidy and predictable than the reality they aim to portray. From what a number of practitioners in the disciple making process have witnessed over the years, it would be entirely accurate for congregations to replace the ubiquitous "all are welcome" signs outside their buildings with stark orange signs worded "Caution: God at work!" There is something subversively unpredictable about being involved in preparing people for transformative ministry in the world. Lives change, and not just those of the inquirers. When a congregation starts taking seriously the vocation to make disciples, its life is bound to change too!

Meet Corey

One brisk November Sunday morning, a seventeen-year-old man named Corey stood before a congregation during the opening part of the liturgy. As an inquirer for over a year, Corey had often leaned forward in his pew marking each sermon's words with determined attention. As the weeks became months, a growing number of parishioners established a supportive relationship with him, including some of the other teenagers who uncharacteristically hauled themselves out of bed on the odd Saturday morning to load boxes at the food bank, or gathered on Friday evenings for frivolous fun, frank faith-sharing, or both. As Advent loomed on the horizon, Corey was now declaring before the congregation his desire to become a follower of Christ.

To the questions posed as part of a rite of welcome (see Preparation for the Rite of Welcome, pages 91-92), Corey offered answers of his own that gripped the hearts of the welcoming congregation. In response to the question, "What do you ask of the church?" Corey responded, "To hear God's word with you and share in your service to those in need."

The impact upon the people in the pews that day was palpable. "I don't think I truly realized just what we share as Christians," one woman remarked with tears welling from her eyes, "until I heard that young man ask to be part of us today." That very week this woman who witnessed Corey's verbal commitment to the church was herself joining one of the congregation's small groups in order to reflect on the scriptures and lend her hands in hospitality to those who were hungry.

As has happened many times before and since in the life of that congregation, the initial steps of deliberate discipleship for one person served to renew many people in the discipleship that was already theirs through baptism. Now, what should the sign outside the church have read that morning? "All are welcome. Come on in!" or "Caution: God at work. Lives may be changed!"

Meet Judy

Then there is the Texas congregation in which Judy, a woman in her late twenties, reflected on scripture. She also cultivated the practice of Christian service by volunteering in local nursing homes. Quickly she became so appalled by the conditions she saw in those facilities that she became an advocate for the rights of seniors, testifying before the state legislature and summoning her congregation to take part in what proved to be the successful lobby for reform in the nursing home industry of Texas. As a result, people who would have otherwise been incapacitated or died received a much higher standard of care, and a congregation was called back to the discipleship that was already theirs through baptism. Caution: God at work. Lives may be changed!

Similar stories could fill the rest of this book: a church restructuring itself into cell groups so everyone could engage in formation patterned after its disciple making process; a suburban faith community filled with elderly worshipers finding fresh purpose as young families coming for baptism remained because of the welcome received and supportive relationships established; another congregation becoming more genuinely open and hospitable after adopting an intentional disciple making process and reversing its decline from when their goal had simply been to attract new members. Caution: God at work. Lives may be changed!

There is no doubt that now is the time for people to take up anew a vocation to make disciples. This book presents a way for the church to come into radical realignment with the life and ministry of Jesus Christ. But beware! Lives will be changed, including your own! Proceed with caution.

Understanding the Process for Making Disciples

People do not only think their way into new modes of behaving, they also behave their way into new understandings and modes of thinking. In any dimension of human life, transformation of understanding, insight, practice, and habit takes time and usually deliberate attention. This dynamic is no less true when it comes to living the life of a Christian disciple.

The Catechumenate: An Ancient Gift Reopened

A process of discipleship formation that fosters and guides conversion into a Christian way of life is often called the *catechumenate* (kat-eh-**kyoo**-meh-net). Strictly speaking, a catechumenate involves only unbaptized seekers, since it offers an intentional approach for incorporating individuals into the body of Christ. The catechumenate is shaped by four stages: *inquiry, exploration, intense preparation,* and *baptismal living.* These are described in this handbook (other presentations of a catechumenal process may use other names for the stages, though the process itself is usually similar). Each stage is built around scripture, prayer, worship, reflection, witness, service, and the introduction to various Christian disciplines and practices. As individuals move through each stage they are supported and accompanied by many members of a congregation who serve as catechists, sponsors, mentors, and friends in faith. The movement from one stage to the next is marked by threshold *rites* that are celebrated in public worship. The overall aim is to form people able to live as Christian disciples in every facet of life.

The model for this pattern of welcoming and forming disciples comes to us from the ancient church, when many Christian communities gave careful attention to people who were being drawn by the Holy Spirit into their way of life. In the earliest centuries, church leaders knew that people seeking to share their life in Christ had to take a series of short steps since the full distance of living among the baptized was simply too great to be made in one leap. Many of our earliest ancestors in faith understood themselves to be participants in the new creation initiated by the resurrection of Jesus Christ. Through baptism they were called to be an alternative order of society profoundly identified with God's promised reign of reconciliation, peace, and justice. They were a company standing in contrast from the values and addictions of conventional society. Therefore the risks and changes belonging to baptism were too great to be undertaken without careful preparation and consideration by both catechumens and community alike.

The ancient model of the catechumenate speaks to many contemporary needs in that the Christian church does not now have the same kind of cultural dominance in North America that it had through even much of the twentieth century. Many people now commonly refer to the current times as a post-Constantinian or post-Christendom era. A significant shift in the church's place within the larger culture seems to call forth a more intentional process of incorporating new followers of Christ.

A Staged Approach to Becoming a Christian

As in the ancient church's approach for a catechumenate, the contemporary stages for approaching baptism with adult seekers are raised by the horizon of baptism itself. In each stage people preparing for baptism are asked key questions related to the issues and focus relevant to their ongoing process of conversion. Their sponsors are called upon to mentor them in this work and to offer testimony to the church regarding their progress and readiness. Meanwhile, all members of the congregation are called upon for support and to renew their own commitment to Christ.

The timing of the stages belonging to this process is critical. People cannot come suddenly to the questions raised in each stage (especially baptism itself) if they have had little or no prior experience of Christian faith, the scriptures, and life with the church. A journey of faith development needs guidance and time in which to experience prayer, learn the stories of salvation, participate in the ministry and worship of the church, and recognize ways of interacting with all of life's opportunities and challenges.

The time frame for the initial stages of a process used in making disciples must unfold in response to the needs and readiness of the people involved. The duration of each stage will vary from individual to individual and need not be linked to any specific program length or season of the liturgical year. Once it has been discerned that a person is ready and willing to celebrate baptism though, the timeline is usually determined more by the church's calendar, itself an expression of Christ's sovereignty over the rhythms of our lives. In this way the time frame of the process becomes another expression of a person's conversion into the life of Christ.

Adapting the Catechumenate for Already Baptized Seekers

In the attempt to restore the catechumenate to our own time, several congregations have discovered that many people who seek a firmer grounding in the life of faith are already Christians (already baptized, that is), but either seek to return to church life as adults or to re-engage their faith in ways that they have not done previously.

Although the catechumenate is a ministry with people seeking baptism, it also has much to teach us about ministry among those who have not been consciously living out baptismal faith in their daily lives. That is why many denominational traditions provide a parallel process (another *track* if you like) for welcoming returning members through (re)affirmation of baptism. This book is written from the standpoint that many congregations will have a mixture of adult disciples to train; people who are yet to be baptized as well as people who have already been baptized.

What cannot be stressed too strongly is that *baptism* (no matter how long ago it might have occurred for a person) *leaves an indelible mark* that needs to be honored and respected in a congregation's process of making disciples. Yet if already baptized people have not ever been well grounded or formed in the Christian faith, many of their spiritual development needs are similar to those who have not been baptized. This book will help you to form a disciple making process in your congregation and work with inquirers and other adults who may have a variety of needs, whether seeking baptism or wanting to affirm baptism in some way.

Please note that newcomers to your congregation who have already been active in the church in another place, particularly within the same denomination or within a tradition with which you may be in full communion, may simply need to transfer their membership to your congregation. Such persons who are already active in church life (or who have recently been so) might not need or be interested in the complete process of making disciples that this book presents. The assumption is that their faith is reasonably mature, but they still need to be introduced to the people and customs of your particular congregation. Of course it should not be assumed that simply because someone is currently on the membership roster of another congregation there is no need for faith formation. Each prospective new member's needs has to be uniquely assessed; something that will be dealt with later in the chapter on Inquiry.

A Ministry of Welcome

In a rite of welcome often used in the disciple making process newcomers are asked "What are you seeking?" This question is not asked to satisfy our curiosity. Instead, the question honors the ones who are being welcomed. In asking this question we indicate that their faith journey matters to us. We want to know what newcomers are seeking because we want to join them in exploring how God is already working in their lives. Asking such a question may be a small thing, but the gesture is part of a much bigger approach to hospitality that puts the needs of our guests first.

Too often, what Christian communities call hospitality is really a process designed to meet their own needs. If we want to survive, we have to grow, some have been known to say. Others try to state the case more subtly, but hospitality driven by the need to gain members is always turned inward. On the other hand, genuine hospitality that is directed first toward the needs of guests takes on an evangelical nature that ends up benefiting the whole community of faith.

Those who welcome people into community through the use of an intentional disciple making process find common ground in three affirmations about hospitality:

1. HOSPITALITY BEGINS WITH LISTENING

Sadly, this has not been the norm in many religious communities that invite newcomers to classes at which they are the listeners and leaders are the only storytellers. The disciple making process presented in this book, though, begins with the church effectively saying, "Tell us who you are and help us understand the questions and the life experiences you bring to us." Instead of coming with a canned curriculum to teach, leaders of the disciple making process allow the stories and questions of the participants to determine the flow of the conversation. When it comes to the study of the Bible we say, "Let us listen to this living Word together and discover how it is speaking to each one of us."

2. HOSPITALITY IS ALWAYS OPEN-ENDED

When the only thing offered to guests is a new member class, the expectations of the host are very clear. Participation means a commitment to join the community. In communities that use the disciple making process, though, participants are welcomed into a faith journey that is open to the Spirit's leading. There is room for all, at whatever point they may be in their journey of faith. Indeed some participants may already know that they want to become members of the host community, but many others are simply looking for a safe space to explore the Christian faith or to discern whether this is where they want to live out their baptismal calling. An invitation to join the community is always extended along the way, and a time for receiving new members is built into the cycle of the disciple making process, but participants are always free to follow where the Spirit is leading them and to do so with the full affirmation of the hosts.

This was true for Tami, who attended a gathering for inquirers that used an intentional disciple making process. As she shared her story and heard God's word with others, Tami began to sense that God was leading her back to another congregation she had left several years earlier. Though she appreciated the love and support that the disciple making process had given to her, through that group's deep listening to her story they allowed her to discover that the best path forward was for her to reconnect with her previous congregation. Nonetheless the disciple making process had done its work by focusing on Tami's call to be a disciple and not simply on the congregation's need to expand its membership. Tami especially appreciated the prayers that the inquiry group offered to her during her last meeting with them.

3. HOSPITALITY IS NEVER RUSHED

One of the most important features of a genuine disciple making process is that it is oriented around the time frame of the participants and not some fixed dates on the church calendar that demand rigid conformity. As Jesus said to Nicodemus, "the wind blows where it chooses … (and) so it is with everyone who is born of the Spirit" (John 3:8). An authentic ministry of welcome takes this into consideration and always allows flexibility in the development of a process that corresponds with the needs of the guests and the timing of God in their lives.

When these three basic practices of hospitality are observed, the whole Christian community learns to become less anxious and more trusting of God's providence and timing in all matters of individual and communal life.

An Overview of the Disciple Making Process ◉

The formation process for each stage in the disciple making process described in this book varies according to the purpose for that stage. In each stage, formation is accomplished through the process of experience followed by reflection, usually in small groups. In experiencing the mystery of what Christ has accomplished and is accomplishing for them, participants may reflect on the meaning of that experience in their own lives.

Stage One: Inquiry

Participants reflect on their own story and the biblical story. Inquirers and team members share their own stories in light of the good news of Christ. Individuals bring questions about God, faith, and the church, while trying to find meaning for their lives.

Stage Two: Exploration

Participants reflect on the Christian life: worship, service, prayer, mission, and community. The basis for much of the discussion and reflection is scripture, particularly as it unfolds through the weekly scripture readings at worship (typically from a lectionary).

Stage Three: Intense Preparation

This is a time of preparing a candidate for baptism or for affirmation of baptism. Candidates explore the baptismal covenant, reflecting on what God promises through baptism and what the believer's response in faith is to be. Four scripture passages from the gospel according to John often form much of the basis for further reflection on the Christian life in this stage: Jesus' meeting with Nicodemus (John 3:1-17), Jesus and the woman at the well (John 4:5-42), the healing of the man born blind (John 9:1-41), and the raising of Lazarus (John 11:1-45). [Note: Most congregations that use a three-year lectionary system encounter these readings during year A of Lent. Congregations that frequently have baptismal candidates during Lent may use these lectionary readings regardless of the year.]

Stage Four: Baptismal Living

Participants reflect on the sacraments of baptism and communion, and on the paschal mystery of Christ's death and resurrection. They explore how these events shape their lives and empower them for ministry in daily life. Other topics for discussion and reflection may include discernment of gifts and opportunities for ministry as believers live out baptism in their daily lives and relationships. The disciple making team guides participants to meaningful associations in the life of the church and its mission in the world.

An Overview of Rites of Discipleship ☙

The celebration of baptism is the climax of becoming a disciple of Jesus. By its very nature it is public and communal, for it celebrates adoption into a new family. It is also countercultural because it is a decisive act of dying to evil powers in order to be raised to new life in Christ. Any attempt to soften this radical claim of baptism will inevitably deny its very essence.

Becoming a disciple of Jesus Christ is not accomplished by a magic ritual. Formation as a disciple is a process that presupposes a personal crisis. If it was not a personal crisis that brought a candidate to seek baptism then the process of becoming a disciple will certainly provoke one! Ideally, baptism will not be celebrated until it is clear to candidates and others that this crisis has been faced. The disciple making process is how the community supports and guides people in dealing with a crisis of faith and growing through it into the life of discipleship.

Because of the public nature of the church, the process of becoming a disciple cannot be entirely private, so specific moments are celebrated with the Christian community. Like baptism itself, they are threshold rituals: they mark moments of growth when a person has begun to deal with part of the challenge of discipleship even while another dimension of the challenge lies ahead.

There are two major threshold rituals that can be experienced before baptism or affirmation of baptism. The first, the **rite of welcome**, comes after a time of inquiry. By this point inquirers will have recognized that the story Christians tell is of genuine interest to them and worth engaging in a serious way. Inquirers will be presented to the congregation at a regular weekly worship service by a member (sponsor) who has agreed to be a companion on this journey of discovery. A pastor or other leader of the community will welcome each inquirer and provide an opportunity for each to say what it is that she or he is seeking. Inquirers are then invited to participate more fully in the life of the church. They will be supported in the congregation's prayers and then signed with the cross. Following this moment, unbaptized inquirers (often called *catechumens* now) as well as candidates for affirmation of baptism will be invited to share with the congregation in hearing God's word and take their places as apprentices in the life of the congregation.

A second major threshold ritual prior to baptism is a **rite of enrollment** as a candidate for baptism. It comes after catechumens have experienced the way of a disciple for a period of time and are convinced that this is the path to which they are committed for the rest of their lives. By this point catechumens are likely more attuned to the unfolding story of Christ as enacted through the liturgical year, and it will now be clear why enrolling candidates for baptism normally occurs at the beginning of Lent, in preparation for baptism at the Vigil of Easter. After the readings and sermon, candidates once again are presented to the congregation. Sponsors speak on behalf of each candidate, recommending them for baptism. Candidates are asked whether they are ready to answer the call of Christ and desire to be baptized. The congregation will affirm their calling, and they will be enrolled (candidate names may actually be entered in a book of enrollment). Prayer will be offered for the candidates as they begin their Lenten journey. Candidates who are preparing for affirmation of baptism may be invited to take part in a rite of continuing conversion, perhaps on Ash Wednesday.

Whatever form a baptismal candidate's crisis of faith has taken, it is a crisis that is enacted through the sacrament of **baptism**. The primary time for receiving adult candidates through baptism is at the Vigil of Easter, the pinnacle of the liturgical year. Beginning with the lighting of a new fire, worshipers will then recall the sweeping saga of the world's salvation through scripture, song, and prayer. The images of creation, salvation from the flood, rescue from ancient terrors, and deliverance from slavery are invoked to illumine the story of Jesus' death and resurrection, for he sacrificed his life to deliver the world from the powers of evil.

Images from the Vigil of Easter liturgy will also illumine baptismal candidates' deliverance from destructive forces. When the action shifts from the world's story to an individual's story, baptismal candidates will be invited to stand and renounce all the evils that have held them captive. This is the climax of the crisis into which following the way of Jesus has plunged a Christian disciple. As baptismal candidates turn their backs on the powers of evil they claim for themselves the freedom that Jesus offers and move toward the baptismal waters. There the community of faith gives thanks for the many ways that God has delivered them through water and will pray for baptismal candidates' deliverance in this moment. Together with all the baptized, the candidates commit themselves to the covenant of baptism, taking their place within the great story of salvation. Baptismal candidates enter the dark waters of death, trusting in God's promise of resurrection and new life. Coming out of the water they may be greeted with shouts of Alleluia; the sign of the cross is marked on their foreheads (accompanied, perhaps, by anointing with oil). The newly baptized will be welcomed into the household of God and called to share in the church's witness to Christ. As new sisters and brothers share the greeting of peace with one another, all the baptized are invited to share in the eucharist, the banquet of the age to come.

What Is Offered to People Who Are Already Baptized? ❂

What is the path for those who are technically Christians but effectively without growth in the Christian faith? Those who are affirming their baptism can be involved in a discipleship process with many of the same features as those preparing for baptism: a welcome after a period of inquiry, followed by a time of apprenticeship with the support of a companion; something like an enrollment at the beginning of Lent once they are prepared to renew their commitments within the covenant of baptism; and a climactic ritual of affirmation (possibly using water as a thanksgiving for baptism, but not baptism itself).

In many ways the whole congregation is invited to follow such a journey throughout the season of Lent, for learning to be a disciple is a journey that only ends in the age to come. So all the baptized are invited to renew that journey: on Ash Wednesday the worshiping assembly is called to a life of conversion, recognizing a communal ongoing crisis of dying to the evils around us through a ceremony of ashes. If people are rejoining the church through affirmation of baptism, their participation in this rite will provide a model for all the baptized who are taking up the journey. On Maundy Thursday, when the church remembers how Jesus stooped to wash his disciples' feet, candidates for baptismal affirmation may participate in this ritual too as a model of restoration to communion through mutual service. Then, when the great celebration of Easter comes, affirmers will share with all the baptized at the Lord's table, rejoicing in the mercy offered to all people through Jesus' death and rising.

In some traditions participants in an affirmation of baptism will also have the opportunity for an affirmation of vocation at some later time, perhaps at Pentecost. An affirmation of vocation is not a threshold rite, but rather a communal recognition of all Christian disciples' ministries as people of God.

Baptized People Are Invited to Discipleship

Because they are already baptized, returning and searching members may participate with candidates for baptism so long as they are never mistaken or treated other than as full and complete members of Christ's body, the church.

- Stages and rites that *parallel* those offered to baptismal candidates may be used with those returning to the baptismal covenant.

- The rites used with returning members recognize and honor a member's baptism and point toward affirmation.

- The resources of the Anglican, Episcopal, Lutheran, Roman Catholic, Presbyterian, and United Methodist churches provide description, guidance, and ritual texts for use with returning members.

Non-member Parents Requesting Baptism for Their Children

When we as a church think about baptism from the perspective of a non-member parent or parental guardian we realize that baptism may seem very much like a onetime event. The water is poured into the font and splashes around; a few words are uttered while some eyes close and others open widely to peer around the room in wonder; finally a sprinkling or a smearing or a dipping or a dunking. The practice of baptism is over and gone in a flash. How do we approach the curiosity? How do we calm the worry? How do we encourage participation far beyond this day?

The disciple making process in this book offers a way to include non-member parents who request baptism for their children. On these occasions families may join together with a number of other inquirers (see the chapter on Inquiry), or there may be specific sessions for non-member families requesting baptism. In this respect congregations may find it easier to affirm the desire that non-member families have for baptism and to offer solid support for them, rather than simply accommodating requests for baptism to be performed quickly and without a meaningful connection to the ongoing life of the church.

A process of making disciples invites church leaders to respect the backgrounds of all seekers, including non-member families requesting baptism for their children, and to listen carefully for any evidence of a spiritual history, without necessarily asking any of the following questions directly. Has the family already been involved in the life of the church in some way? Has a family member ever been hurt or deeply disappointed by the church? Did the family grow up in a home with many strict religious traditions or in a home largely unaffected by religious customs and teachings? Parents should be assured that their stories are valued. There are many reasons why they may have been on the periphery of church life until now. They may also need to hear that practices that once existed in various congregations and denominations are not necessarily representative of the church today. Questions about faith—even doubts—are encouraged.

The process of making disciples offers the possibility of faith formation for a whole family. At baptism we hear of God's promises; all people are invited to claim those promises as our own. In meeting with non-member parents who request baptism for their children, church leaders can do a number of things:

- Help the non-member parent or guardian realize that it truly is an impossible thing to fully understand God's covenant with the world, but that it is a lifelong process;

- Tell the non-member parent or guardian confidently that baptism is a visible sign of God's invisible grace working in us and in the world; and

- Promise the non-member parent or guardian full sponsorship and acceptance in the life of the church.

When a congregation is faithful to the covenant of baptism, it finds ways to interact with the family even after baptism. Whether a parent or guardian understands it or not, the covenant of God has permeated their family system. It means that his or her child has been protected and prompted by something larger and that baptism in Christ lays a claim on a person throughout all of life.

When non-member parents are invited into a process of becoming disciples themselves, they can discover how baptism can be both a onetime event and forever.

Getting Started

Why Be Involved in Making Disciples?

Meet Sharon

After worship one Sunday, the pastor came out of his office to find a visitor standing in the narthex. It was the first time Sharon had attended a service at this church and now she was the only one left in the building. The pastor greeted her and asked if she needed anything. She said, "I'm looking for something." "What are you looking for?" the pastor asked, thinking of a misplaced purse or sweater. She said, "I don't really know. I don't even know why I came here today. All I know is I'm looking for something."

I'm looking for something. How would you and your congregation respond to such a statement? We can assume that many people are seeking God and that hearts are restless until they find rest in God. We can also assume that people who are seeking will need support and encouragement to take the journey of discovery that is the life of faith. We can also assume that your congregation is exactly the right place for this journey to take place and the right community to accompany seekers in the way of Christ.

Upon describing the process of exploring the Christian faith with other seekers, of being accompanied and supported as she tested the waters, Sharon received an invitation. It was an invitation to get to know Jesus and his church. Was she interested in this? Closing her eyes and taking a deep breath, she exhaled: Yes!

This is how Sharon came to know and love Jesus and to enter more deeply into relationship with him. As with any new relationship, she was given the freedom to explore and try on the faith. A congregation offered her the opportunity to ask questions of Jesus and his church, to bring to the relationship issues that had confounded, confused, or annoyed her. Simultaneously, the church introduced Sharon to the scriptures, the sacraments, prayer, life in community, service to the poor, and worship: all gifts by which the church receives Jesus Christ, its one priceless treasure and love. In this way Sharon came to the waters of baptism and the anointing of the Spirit. A life in love of God and service to God's people emerged.

And there is more! As the congregation explored treasures that a seeker desired, longtime members of the church dusted them off and saw them anew. The congregation also came to a deeper relationship with Jesus. Indeed that congregation is continually renewed by seekers coming to know Jesus, as they bring new and inspiring perspectives on the life of the baptized.

Meet Beth

Beth, a newly baptized member, lay sleeping in the hospital bed after a grueling surgery to remove a cancerous tumor. Her pastor and Sandy, her catechist in the disciple making process, stood on either side of the bed, waiting for Beth to wake up. She awoke and smiled at her two visitors. Typically people will begin by saying, "Thanks for coming to see me." Not Beth. Almost next to death, Beth beamed and said, "Look! The two people who were at my side when I was baptized! And now you are here at my side again! It is always death and new life, isn't it?" Here was a newly baptized child of God who *got it* and then gave back to people who had accompanied her on a faith journey not long before.

Why would your congregation want to have a structured process for making Christian disciples? In order to welcome and accompany people like Sharon, Beth, and a host of others who fall in love with Jesus and his church, and who will inspire your congregation to fall in love with being disciples of Jesus Christ all over again.

Meet Courtney

Courtney approached the front doors of the church cautiously. Though they seemed big and heavy to her, her heart felt heavier. The weighty decision before her needed to be talked out between her and God. Whenever her mother had an important decision to make she would walk to the neighborhood church for worship, but Courtney had never been to church. As she made her way through the doors a person with a friendly smile greeted her, handed her a program, and ushered her through another set of doors into the warm worship space. The cold of the winter air outside dissipated as she made her way to a pew. She sat quietly and listened for God in the stillness around her.

After a minute someone tapped Courtney on the shoulder. A bit startled, she looked up to see a gentle smile. The man asked her if she was visiting. She nodded, unsure of whether she should reveal her status. The man then introduced himself as Rodney, a member of the congregation who participated in a process of welcoming newcomers called The Journey. He asked her if she had any requests for prayer that he would hold in his silent prayers during worship. Courtney couldn't imagine saying the words of her request. She shook her head politely. The man smiled again and said, "Okay, I'll keep you in prayer during worship today. What's your name?" Courtney shared her name with a smile and relaxed a little. As Rodney left to return to his pew Courtney's heart warmed a bit.

As worship began Courtney's thoughts shifted from the weight of her decision to following along with what was happening around her. A few minutes into the sermon Courtney's eyes fell to an announcement in the bulletin.

Are you on The Journey?

We welcome you to Cedarbrook Church today. Do you have some-
thing going on in your life you'd like to share with people like you?
We've each shared our stories with someone else in this congrega-
tion and as a result found a home for our questions about faith, as
well as words to describe our encounters with Jesus Christ. We'd
like you to journey with us. Please speak with someone wearing a
green "We're on The Journey" shirt if you'd like more information
or if you'd like to share a prayer request. If today isn't good, leave
your phone number or e-mail address with one of us and we'll con-
tact you later in the week.

Courtney looked up to where Rodney was sitting. She hadn't noticed his green shirt. She wondered whether she'd have the nerve to talk with him after worship. For the time being though she settled back and listened to the sermon.

Two years earlier Rodney had been welcomed by Fred in the same way. Fred's phone call later in the week had led to coffee, which in turn led to Rodney partici- pating in The Journey at Cedarbrook Church. Fred had even been assigned as Rod- ney's sponsor. Over the weeks of reflecting on scripture together, praying, worship- ing, and serving together through The Journey, Rodney and Fred learned each oth- er's stories. Fred had been born into Cedarbrook Church and had served in nearly every capacity the congregation offered. But what was most meaningful to Rodney was that Fred had served in the army like Rodney's dad. There were moments when Rodney could almost hear his dad's voice when Fred would give him some advice.

One evening Fred asked Rodney to pray for him. Fred's wife had been undergo- ing medical tests and had been diagnosed with cancer. Fred seemed quite shaken. Rodney asked Fred what Jesus had to do with all this. Rodney would never forget Fred's response. He looked up and said, "Rodney, Jesus has everything to do with this moment, right here." At that moment the stories about Jesus that Rodney had been hearing week after week on The Journey flooded his imagination. Even though Fred said nothing more, Rodney realized his desire to be baptized at Cedarbrook Church.

Rodney saw Courtney sit down in the pew that Sunday morning. Before he approached Courtney, Rodney looked over at Fred, who was now sitting alone in

Go Make Disciples

the pew. He would join him in a moment, but first he wanted to check on this visitor. Rodney tapped her on the shoulder and smiled.

Why Should We Do This?

Learning to welcome seekers in your congregation may take some time and conversation among congregational leaders. Here are some ways to think about how a process of making disciples could contribute to your congregation's life:

- This is *an open-ended yet structured process* that welcomes individuals, attends to their stories, and cultivates a specifically Christian faith identity for the spiritual but not religious seeker.

- Newcomers and congregational disciples will gather together regularly to share and reflect upon the core narrative of Jesus Christ.

- The methods encountered here involve recurring practices—faith forming and sustaining practices of scripture reading, praying, worship, and serving—that are infused with meaning as they are embodied in the community's practice and lead to congregational renewal.

- This process encourages active newcomer participation in the life of faith and fosters interaction between newcomers and disciples.

- This process is a practice of discipleship particularly helpful for mainline Protestants who aren't sure how to form new disciples and renew lifelong discipleship.

- This process is missional as it looks for where Jesus of Nazareth is already ahead of us bringing about the reign of God.

Depending on the role you bear in your congregation, you will bring different concerns as you try to decide whether or not to introduce a disciple making process in your congregation:

- You may serve on the evangelism committee, so questions about evangelism, welcoming newcomers, and hospitality may be central to your concern.

- You may be a parent whose young adult child doesn't come to church anymore and you are looking for a way to welcome young adults—perhaps even your own—in your congregation.

- You may serve on the stewardship committee or be a spiritual gifts coordinator, so questions about practicing faith in relation to daily life are central.

- You may serve as a congregational leader who loves your congregation, and you wish to see its renewal in a life of faith.

- You may be a director of Christian Education for whom questions about engaging scripture, renewing faith, and discipleship formation take priority.

- You may be a pastor who is interested in congregational mission and renewal, or perhaps you desire to welcome newcomers with a process that has origins in the history of the early church and its sacramental practices.

- Perhaps you have been a sponsor, inquirer, or affirmer in the past and are now eager to learn more about the disciple making process.

Reread some of the ways to think about the disciple making process listed above. Which of these statements speaks to your concerns for the church of Jesus Christ and for your congregation?

———————————————————————

Following are some additional thoughts about why congregations should practice an intentional process of making disciples based on the ancient and newly-revived catechumenate. Hopefully one might speak to the concerns that are central to your congregation or your role in the church.

THE PROCESS IS CENTERED ON JESUS CHRIST

Pluralism as the coexistence of multiple ethnic, racial, religious, and social groups is a growing phenomenon in North America. More than ever North Americans are encountering people of different religious traditions in their daily interactions or even within their own families. Pluralism has implications for congregations in two ways:

- First, newcomers to a congregation may come having experience with a variety of religious traditions and may not be sure how to situate themselves comfortably within one particular religious tradition such as Christianity. Sociologists call these people who stand at the edge of a faith *liminals*. As *Go Make Disciples* will make clear, this process draws seekers into the particular story of Jesus Christ through regular engagement with scripture, prayer, and regular participation in worship and service. Congregations that share the core narrative of faith consistently over time will cultivate a particular Christian faith identity among North American liminals.

- Second, people already participating in the congregation, perhaps like yourself, may also identify with liminals at times. This process draws newcomers, as well as the sponsors and catechists who guide them, into the renewal of your congregation's commitment to a life centered in Jesus Christ.

NEWCOMERS AND MATURE DISCIPLES PRACTICE FAITH TOGETHER

New learning paradigms are active and participatory. Walk into a third grade classroom in North America and you will witness students' active participation in learning activities and rich interactive learning between peers. Or observe a retirement community's video game bowling event or a group heading off on an Elderhostel adventure and you will see evidence of interactive participation and learning at the same time.

This is an ancient process that encourages active newcomer participation in the life of faith and fosters interaction between newcomers and disciples. The disciple making process doesn't talk *about* faith with newcomers. The process *practices* faith. The process engages newcomers together with other disciples through scripture, prayer, worship, and service. The process keeps central the practices of Christian faith that form disciples of Jesus Christ and leads congregations toward a renewal of commitment for missional life in the world God loves.

MAKING DISCIPLES IS MISSIONAL

At the end of the gospel according to Mark, a young man dressed in white spoke to the women who had come to the tomb where Jesus' body had been to anoint him. The young man said, "Do not be alarmed; you are looking for Jesus of Nazareth, who was crucified. He has been raised; he is not here. Look, there is the place they laid him. But go, tell his disciples and Peter that he is going ahead of you to Galilee; there you will see him, just as he told you" (Mark 16:6-7). Jesus Christ is way ahead of us, attending to those who do not yet follow him, preparing hearts, minds, bodies, and souls to live life as his faithful disciples.

The process of making disciples is missional as it looks for where Jesus of Nazareth is already ahead of us bringing about the reign of God. Catechists, sponsors, and the whole congregation join the young man at Jesus' tomb inviting all who inquire to join the journey toward Galilee. In this way the process of making disciples centers the congregation's life in God's missional impulse to love the entire world.

Why Should the Congregation Care about Making Disciples?

ISN'T THIS THE PASTOR'S JOB?

Newcomer classes in many congregations are often scheduled with the pastor. For many people it seems as though the pastor can best address the faith questions of newcomers. The process that is described in this book is based on the ancient and newly-revived catechumenate and it approaches welcoming newcomers rather differently. This process relies on the involvement of a number of regular participants within the congregation. Especially in congregations that may be used to the pastor being the most important person involved in welcoming newcomers, this method of making disciples may seem odd in its emphasis on developing relationships between newcomers and members in the congregation; however, welcoming newcomers shouldn't be the pastor's job alone.

It's often easy for regular participants in the life of a congregation to imagine who to go to with a specific question about a life of faith. For a newcomer, however, discerning whom to approach is a challenge. While the pastor is an obvious choice, there is often a group of people already surrounding that leader waiting to have a word. A newcomer might also wonder whether it is even appropriate to ask the pastor some basic question. How much easier might it be to approach someone who looks approachable? Or how much easier might it be if the newcomer was the one approached?

The contributors to this book acknowledge that welcoming people into the life of a congregation is a task belonging to the whole church, not just to a cadre of folks who receive advanced training and are employed by it.

Is the Congregation Ready to Do This?

Whether you step carefully through this book, tracing your finger across each word with determined concentration, or simply skip gingerly along fanning through its pages with your thumb, there is something you will probably notice: the contributors to this volume are convinced that cultivating a process of making disciples can yield a bountiful harvest in congregations. Even if you find this enthusiasm contagious, you may feel a little cautious too. Can this process really succeed in my congregation? Are the people here ready for this? Do we have what it takes to pull it off?

These are crucial considerations. After all, *Go Make Disciples* does not simply describe one program to set alongside any number of others. It has the potential to reshape the whole manner of how we *do* church. It certainly requires active commitment on the part of a significant number of people in a congregation. So here are some questions to ponder in discerning your faith community's readiness for this process. If you answer a question with a confident *yes*, move on to the next. If not, have a look at the suggestions beneath the query. They may be just what you need to prepare your congregational soil and plant a number of fruitful seeds.

IS OURS A ROBUST CELEBRATION OF BAPTISM?

The manner in which we worship, for better or for worse, shapes us as individuals and communities. How we celebrate baptism must embody, not contradict, its meanings and importance. So, to ensure your answer to this question will be yes, start with the following:

- Never celebrate private baptisms (except in emergencies). All baptisms are rightfully celebrations of the faith community and should be held when its members gather for Sunday worship.

- Reserve baptisms for the great baptismal festivals: the Vigil of Easter, Pentecost, All Saints Day, and the Baptism of Our Lord. If you are blessed with an abundance of baptisms over the course of a year, add another baptismal festival in late summer (perhaps near the Transfiguration of Our Lord on August 6 for Episcopalians and Anglicans). Congregations of some denominations will also want to set aside Sundays on which the bishop pays a visit. These occasions anchor the understanding and appreciation of baptism in the rhythms of a congregation's life.

- Use plenty of jubilant music in baptismal services. You can never sing too many "alleluias" on such occasions. Baptisms are a big deal, so celebrate!

- Make lavish use of symbols and gestures. Use lots of water and lots of scented oil. Also use real bread for communion (and if it's baked in the church kitchen, hopefully the smell will fill the worship space). Encourage members of the congregation to extend their hands during the welcome or blessing of the newly baptized.

- Ensure that a period of communal preparation takes place before baptisms. Baptismal preparation should involve more than just the pastor and the candidate or parents of an infant candidate. This preparation should not simply be instructional. The building of trusting relationships is vital not only for incorporating others into the household of faith but also in the formation of disciples for the work of initiation.

- In the spirit of the previous suggestion, prepare and provide baptismal sponsors from your congregation. The time, interest, and caring of people is the greatest gift you can offer those who are searching or seeking to grow closer to Christ. It usually proves to be a great gift too for the sponsors themselves (see Identifying Sponsors in the chapter on Inquiry, pages 87-88).

DOES OUR CONGREGATION TREAT THE PREFERRED DAYS FOR BAPTISM AS TRUE FESTIVALS?

As noted above, these occasions reinforce the meanings and importance of baptism in a church's life. Their observance demonstrates the priority a faith community places upon baptism. Marking them over time awakens a congregation's awareness of and enthusiasm for vigorous baptismal practice. Therefore, even if there is no celebration of baptism on these days:

- Make sure to include the renewal of baptismal vows or a thanksgiving for baptism in the service. Keep the congregation's focus on God's promises and on its identity as expressed in baptism.

- Ensure the same level of jubilant music and lavish use of symbols as in your celebrations of baptism. For example, after worshipers have renewed their vows, sprinkle them with water from the font or have them approach the font themselves to run their hands through the water and trace the sign of the cross on their foreheads. Have everyone sing "alleluia" or a simple uplifting refrain as they do this.

- Observe baptismal anniversaries for members of the congregation. Over time these will grow, particularly around the traditional baptismal festival days. Send each person a card, perhaps with an invitation to the service at which his or her baptism will be remembered. Have a cake for baptismal anniversaries in the social hour following worship.

- Treat the whole day (not just the worship services) as a celebration. Hold a barbeque or banquet. Provide intergenerational activities in the afternoon that focus on baptism in light of the particular festival day. Offer special events in the evening as a gift to the wider community.

ARE THE CONGREGATION'S GROUPS, ESPECIALLY ITS LEADERSHIP, ALREADY BEING SHAPED BY A DISCIPLE MAKING PROCESS?

The degree of discipleship that you can expect with newcomers is commensurate with the degree of discipleship evident among members.

- Make sure every group is engaged with the building blocks of discipleship: worship, prayer, scripture reflection, and service. For example, if you lead an outreach or service group, provide time for people to share in prayer and scripture reflection. Likewise, prayer and worship groups should be engaged in some act of service beyond themselves.

- Pattern existing study groups after one of the methods offered in Scripture Reflection Methods in this book's Additional Resources chapter (pages 140-143).

- Introduce your leaders to the competencies necessary for a fruitful process of making disciples. For example, a congregation's council, board, session, or vestry could augment its standard devotional moment with a twenty-minute faith sharing exercise or scripture reflection. After several months of this, leaders in the congregation are better prepared to speak naturally about their faith with others in and beyond the church. Other committees and groups in the congregation could pattern their devotional time in the same way.

IS THE CONGREGATION YEARNING TO BE MORE EFFECTIVE
IN ITS MINISTRY TO THOSE SEEKING BAPTISM?

There is a big difference between a congregation that feels impatient because baptisms interrupt their worship life and those who are impatient with their own failure to minister effectively to baptismal candidates or their families. In addition to the suggestions above, you can kindle this desire in your congregation as you:

- Consistently communicate a baptismal vision for your congregation. Use preaching (see A Word to Preachers, pages 159-161), Bible studies, newsletters, blogs, and posts on social media sites. Even home visits can provide opportunities to talk about people's experience of baptism.

- Help people connect the dots. Point out the natural connections between an intentional disciple making process and what the congregation is doing already.

- Highlight for teams or groups in your congregation how their work flows from baptism. Be particularly attentive to this in regard to lectionary texts, hymns, or orders of worship from the previous or upcoming Sunday.

- Gather into a small group those who ache for a more effective baptismal practice. As they consider how baptismal formation might be improved in your church they will stumble upon fresh insights, pose key questions, and accurately gauge your congregation's receptivity. They will also discover and model the shared ministry upon which an effective disciple making process depends.

IS THE PASTOR RECEPTIVE TO MAKING DISCIPLES?

Making disciples need not be a clergy-driven process; however, the pastor's support and involvement is crucial over the long term.

- Provide the pastor with a copy of this book.

- Take into account your pastor's style of working. Honest conversation will suggest next steps with your pastor. Don't assume resistance. Look for common ground in dialogue and how you can be supportive of your pastor. Listen openly to your pastor's concerns, frustrations, joys, and aspirations. Share your perspective and hopes in a gentle but enthusiastic way. If you are part of the congregation's leadership team, are there responsibilities from which your pastor might be relieved to allow her or his participation in a fruitful process of supporting the development of disciples?

- If you are presently searching for a new pastor, make sure this process of making disciples is named as a priority or aspiration for your congregation.

- Identify what you can do to support making disciples in your area of ministry.

- Find companions with whom you can gather. You may find that you can become leaven within your congregation. Together with others you can discover fresh insights and model the shared ministry upon which the making of disciples depends.

There may be some resistance as you act on the suggestions above. However, patient but purposeful persistence can lead a congregation to embrace its vocation to discipleship and faithfully respond to the spiritual hunger of the seekers it welcomes. Take small, measured steps. Allow disciple making practices to evolve. Provide time for people to reflect on new experiences. Celebrate and build on successes. These elements all help to prepare the fertile soil in which a fruitful process of making disciples can take root and grow.

Evangelization and Making Disciples

There is a cartoon that depicts a pastor at the church door motioning to someone passing by and saying, "Come on in." The bystander replies, "Come on out!" For too long the church has been preoccupied with trying to find ways to get unchurched people in the front door of the church. The new paradigm shift is to go where the people are. It is to send out legions of disciples from our communities of faith to serve as front line missionaries and share the good news of Jesus.

In his book, *Borderland Churches*, Gary Nelson offers his vision of the church as a borderland people, living out their faith in the world as the sent people of God. He writes, "The borderland church understands that it is primarily a missional community of people being trained and equipped to live among the world as missionaries. Borderland Christians see their primary role as missionaries."

This is in some ways the task of evangelization that precedes an invitation to join in the disciple making process of faith formation. The church is sent out into the world to partner in God's mission of healing and redemption. The members of our faith communities are called to engage their friends and colleagues in the workplace and the neighborhood while embodying a Christlike spirit in their encounters with others. Some call this *relational evangelism*—naturally sharing our faith in word and deed with others. The new paradigm for the church today is really a return to the book of Acts where we understand that:

- Every member is a missionary.

- Every pastor is a mission director.

- Every congregation is a mission training center.

When those who are unchurched come into contact with modern-day disciples and missionaries from our congregations, will they encounter the risen Christ and a graceful God they may not even know they have yearned for? This becomes the pivotal moment when the invitation to come and see may be most compelling. The seeker is invited to become an inquirer, the first movement of a journey toward faith. Of course there may be those within the community of faith who also yearn to go deeper in their faith walk and learn more about baptismal living—living in the covenant of God's baptismal promise. They too may be invited to join in this spiritual journey of making and becoming disciples, perhaps as affirmers or as sponsors.

What is the hoped-for outcome of this process? "Discipleship is all about helping God's people connect their faith and their gifts with God's mission in the world.

Discipleship doesn't stop at the doors of the church; it isn't concerned only with what goes on inside a congregation. Rather, the focus of the congregation is on strengthening the community of faith for service in God's mission in the world. Discipleship is about bearing witness to the kingdom of God by pursuing truth, justice, mercy, peace, and love in the world." (From Rick Rouse and Craig Van Gelder, *A Field Guide for the Missional Congregation: Embarking on a Journey of Transformation.*)

Encouraging Relational Evangelism

An overwhelmingly large percentage of people (by some accounts between 75 and 90 percent) are newcomers to congregations through personal associations that current members already have with friends, neighbors, relatives, and colleagues. While some people may enter church life in response to an ad, a flyer, or an Internet search, quite likely a personal relationship with an existing member will be the greatest source of newcomers to a congregation.

The following are some ideas that a number of congregations use to encourage current members to be evangelists:

- Hold invite-a-friend Sundays to which members are encouraged to invite others to worship on that day or to various fellowship events or special activities.

- Often people may find it easier (and less of an overt form of proselytizing) if they are encouraged to invite friends and relatives to concerts or social occasions than to worship services or Bible studies.

- Consider how various seasonal events (Christmas programs, Easter egg hunts, ice cream socials, picnics, animal blessings, CROP walks, etc.) may be ways for current members to encourage non-member friends and relatives to attend congregational functions without expecting that they will be committing themselves to anything else. [Note: Inviting guests to these types of events should not be considered as marketing; these events are simply ends to themselves and opportunities to open the church's doors more widely in service to the wider community. Nevertheless, someone who is a guest at a special event might consider that congregation in the future when there is a spiritual need.]

- Print promotional postcards or flyers about various events for current members and worshipers to hand to others.

- Help members of your congregation to see that relational evangelism is something that builds on a person's existing network of relationships. Rather than having to sell the church or market the faith consciously, members are simply witnessing to the importance of faith and of church connections in their own lives. Then when a friend has a concern about a spiritual matter on his or her own timetable, that person might consider a member of the congregation to be a helpful resource. It's a subtle form of evangelism, but it is effective.

Starting a Disciple Making Team

ROLES AND EXPECTATIONS

Making disciples can take place in congregations of any size. Large congregations may have multiple disciple making teams including dozens of people, while smaller congregations may have only a handful of people for a single team, therefore the roles described in this section are not necessarily each to be held by a separate person. Some roles can be combined. Nevertheless, these are descriptions of the various tasks performed by the team members regardless of the number of people on the team.

TEAM LEADER

- Is a lay person who leads in recruiting the team and is the liaison between the team and the congregational leadership, especially the pastor.

- Leads meetings of the disciple making team.

- Represents the disciple making process to the congregation, often taking a role in the various rites of the disciple making process during public worship.

- Assists as a catechist, if gifted in that way, but need not serve in that role.

CATECHIST(S)

- Designs and leads instructional times during disciple making sessions.

- Is familiar with various models of biblical reflection and story sharing.

- Clearly understands the difference between this process and more lecture-style teaching methods.

- Understands that formation is not merely the imparting of information by an expert, but the discovery by participants as a group of what God is doing and where God is leading them.

- Is comfortable with letting teachable moments arise in the process rather than following a set curriculum.

SMALL GROUP LEADERS

- Enable small groups to work effectively.

- Lead groups in scripture reflection and sharing of personal stories by modeling the process, clarifying procedures, and holding the group to norms such as confidentiality and ensuring that all members of the groups have an equal opportunity to contribute and share.

- Take part in planning and evaluating the process and also have an important role in discerning and reporting the experience of the participants to the team.

- Facilitate without dominating and resist answering questions directly, but enable groups to explore possibilities on their own.

- Communicate the need for a formal teaching moment about a specific topic to the catechist(s).

- Are the most important team members, next to sponsors, in the pastoral care of participants.

LITURGY COORDINATOR

- Serves as a liaison to the congregation's worship committee.

- Has thorough knowledge of the rites used in the disciple making process and is responsible for guiding and planning for these liturgical rites, leads rehearsals for them, and may act as a director of liturgy on these occasions.

- Works with presiding and assisting ministers as well as other worship leaders in planning and carrying out rites of the disciple making process.

- Leads prayers and services associated with group sessions and recruits others to partner in this responsibility as well.

MINISTRY COORDINATOR

- Is a liaison to the congregation's outreach ministry (might be a deacon in congregations that have one).

- Provides participants (candidates) in the process with a variety of opportunities to engage in justice or service ministries with the poor and neglected.

- Helps participants identify their gifts and discern how those gifts can be used in ministry through their daily life settings.

Go Make Disciples

RETREAT COORDINATOR

- Takes the lead in planning, scheduling, and coordinating retreats and quiet days throughout the stages of the process.

- Works with other members of the team to plan retreats.

- Schedules the use of retreat spaces in the church building or makes arrangements for another location if a retreat takes place away from the congregation's property.

- Coordinates with congregations' leaders if more than one congregation is joining in a retreat.

PUBLICIST(S)

- Is skilled in various means of communications, printed and electronic.

- Keeps the disciple making process visible and available to the congregation and to visitors year round, often through the use of eye-catching posters and flyers in highly visible locations.

- Designs a page for the congregation's Web site, and uses blogs and social media networks to communicate with all participants and to make the process visible to others.

HOSPITALITY COORDINATOR

- Plans for snacks (or meals) and beverages at every session in order to establish hospitality and a pleasant environment.

- Recruits people to prepare for, serve, and clean up from refreshment times, involving people beyond the disciple making team when possible.

- Lines up food providers well in advance and gives providers timely reminders of the day they are providing food.

SPONSOR COORDINATOR

- Recruits sponsors for participants in the process in consultation with the participants themselves and with other team members in order to see that every participant is paired with an appropriate sponsor.

- Trains sponsors and supports them in their roles.

SPONSORS

- Serve as companions in a one-on-one relationship with every participant throughout the process (from inquiry through baptismal living). Sponsors are already members of the congregation, not the spouses of participants with whom they are paired, and generally of the same gender.

- Serve as guides, friends, and fellow pilgrims to one given person at a time in the process.

- Offer support to participants from the inquiry stage (at least before the rite of welcome) by: (1) sharing all process activities with participants; (2) participating in liturgies with participants; (3) meeting separately with their respective catechumens or candidates on occasion to reflect on the experience; and (4) providing feedback to the disciple making team about participants' experiences in the process.

- Present participants to the congregation at public liturgies.

- Are active members of the congregation, willing to be trained for their role, and willing to attend sessions regularly with their respective participants.

SUPPORT TEAM MEMBERS

- Offer special assistance in areas of expertise, particularly because of biblical or theological training, guidance in prayer and spirituality practices, or ministry discernment gifts.

PASTOR

A pastor is ordinarily another member of the team (see The Pastor's Role in the Disciple Making Process, pages 58-60). Most congregations have found it helpful for lay people to take primary responsibility for leading and staffing the disciple making process though. There are a number of reasons for this:

- The witness and example of non-ordained persons as teachers, worship leaders, small group leaders, and evangelists is essential in forming new baptized members who can develop competencies in those ministries.

- When a pastor takes the lead in the process it is too easy for it to be viewed as that pastor's program, which might well end at the conclusion of that person's tenure.

- The pastor has a significant role in the process as the one who presides and preaches at public liturgies, offers pastoral care to the entire congregation (including participants in the disciple making process), and provides general oversight and support to this and other ministries.

The Pastor's Role in the Disciple Making Process

Many pastors are good leaders and teachers and are likely to answer any question asked of them. As pastors work with the disciple making process they will find it helpful to lead in mostly a collaborative fashion, in order to assist in Christian formation without stifling participants, various team leaders, or the Holy Spirit.

These are some important roles for pastors to fill in a disciple making congregation:

SPIRITUAL LEADER

- The pastor's role in the process is to be a spiritual leader to all participants in the process. This means that when team members are faced with pastoral issues they do not feel competent to deal with on their own, they can turn to a pastor for guidance.

- The pastor may be helpful when issues arise between participants or team members that need intervention.

- The pastor may provide general oversight to the team leader and receive periodic reports from the team leader about the various participants and team members.

- The pastor may assist the team leader in recruiting a team and be consulted when needed on the selection of sponsors for specific participants.

TEACHER OF THE TEACHERS

- Offering their skills as teachers, clergy may be involved in training and supporting the leadership team rather than in leading disciple making sessions themselves.

- Pastors may assist catechists in designing group sessions and in training leaders in models of scripture reflection and story sharing.

- When the team discerns that some formal teaching about scripture, creeds, or worship is needed, they may turn to a pastor for that teaching or to help find another qualified person to do that teaching.

ENABLER OF MINISTRY

- The pastor assists catechists and ministry coordinators in providing a meaningful setting where participants can perform social service and justice work.

- The pastor (and deacon when there is one) should be readily available to the ministry coordinator of the team to help develop and identify good areas of ministry activities and good sources of training for particular ministry skills.

- A pastor's preaching can be greatly enhanced if she or he continually points out the call of the baptized people of God to reach out beyond parish boundaries to those in need and those being denied justice in the wider community.

LITURGICAL PRESIDER

- The pastor presides at the rites marking the stages of the disciple making process. In traditions that have bishops, the pastor presides as the bishop's representative when the bishop cannot be present.

- At rites of the disciple making process, the pastor can embody a loving welcome into deeper life in Christ and fuller appreciation for the gifts of God.

- During preaching at rites of the disciple making process, a pastor can offer guidance to participants about their life as disciples and proclaim a common baptismal identity and witness to the entire congregation.

- Through careful planning and rehearsal, pastoral leadership during rites marking disciples' journeys may employ meaningful gestures that are clearly visible to all (also see Rehearsing the Rites, pages 156-158).

PREACHER

- Pastors preach, teach, and prepare the congregation to serve as an evangelizing and baptizing community. The restoration of the ancient catechumenate has revealed to the churches that our common mission is more than being chaplaincies for the already converted.

- The preacher proclaims that baptism calls the church to its commission to proclaim the good news to all people, making them disciples and leading them to the sacrament of baptism.

- Sermons and teaching may regularly present the Christian life as leading all the baptized into spreading the good news by word and deed.

- The disciple making process in a congregation needs continued preaching of baptism and evangelism as its underlying foundation.

BAPTISMAL LIVING

- Pastors need to be attentive to developing their preaching skills in order to assist congregations to reflect meaningfully on their journeys of faith.

- *Mystagogy* is the historic term for opening up stories and images from the sacred texts (particularly those central to God's salvation of humankind) and for preaching about the sacraments in ways that shed meaning and purpose to the baptized in their ministries of service.

- Preachers will note that especially during the fifty days of the Easter season, scripture readings from the three-year lectionary are meant to open up how our lives can reveal God's love to the world for whom Christ has died and in whom Christ is being continually raised.

Recruiting and Training Team Members

Team members are chosen and invited because of demonstrated skills and gifts they have for these ministries. For this reason it is often counterproductive to make general appeals for anyone to volunteer themselves for these ministries.

- The disciple making team leader needs to be chosen first by the congregation's leadership, and then that leadership works with the team leader to discern persons with the gifts, skills, and temperament to perform the specific roles. In recruiting, those being invited to perform one of the roles need to have a clear understanding of what is expected of them and what level of commitment is needed.

- Most importantly, anyone invited to be on the disciple making team needs to have a clear understanding of baptism and what God has done for them in baptism. Disciple making team members need to share an enthusiasm for bringing newcomers into the life of Christ and for assisting already baptized people to rediscover the gifts of their own baptism. Look especially among people who have recently renewed their own baptismal commitment.

- It is essential to distinguish between formation and indoctrination. People who think in lecture-style terms of imparting information from experts to others need to be introduced to the concept that God implants knowledge in all of us as a community of faith.

- Spend substantial time in the training for each disciple making team member to share the story of his or her pilgrimage in faith. Involve team members in a variety of scripture reflection models (see Scripture Reflection Methods, pages 140-143) over the course of team training.

- Invite disciple making team members to share their discoveries of how God has "hidden . . . things from the wise and intelligent and has revealed them to infants" (Matt. 11:25), and how God opens more to them in reflection and shared stories with others.

- Provide a copy of *Go Make Disciples* (this book) to each disciple making team member. It will also be helpful for each disciple making team or congregation to have a copy of the companion CD-ROM ✪ to this book, so that materials intended to be distributed to participants may be copied from that resource.

- At times disciple making leaders will realize that someone they were recruiting does not have the ability to help guide participants as catechists, small group leaders, or sponsors, but that they may nonetheless serve some of the logistical tasks that are needed.

- Here is also a place where those who preach and teach can enhance training by helping disciple making team members to recognize who and whose they are because of their baptism, their participation in the sacramental life of the church, and their service to the risen Christ through the lives of the poor and helpless with whom they minister.

Leadership Skills

There are two opposite extremes in how leaders act:

AUTOCRATIC All decisions are made by this leader, who, by the fine art of manipulation, may even give the impression that others are involved. The key is control. A group led by an autocratic leader is less likely to be productive in any work it chooses, and the group itself may disintegrate. The autocratic leader may do well in situations where short term productivity or accomplishing a task is the primary objective.

LAISSEZ FAIRE A *laissez faire* leader lays back and lets the group do as it will, without offering any kind of norms for operating, never checking for consensus, and offering very little leadership. Under this kind of leader little is decided. The group is likely to wither and die.

Both of these styles of leadership have merit in certain situations. In practice, the style of the leader will vary somewhere between the two extremes. The task, time, and level of involvement of group members will affect the style.

A third style, half way between the first two, is one toward which an effective leader (especially in the disciple making process) might strive.

MAIEUTIC A Socratic process of assisting a person to bring out into clear consciousness conceptions previously latent in the mind. *Maieutic* (may-**yoo**-tick) also describes the midwife. The midwife does not herself give birth, but makes birth easier by providing support, comfort, ideas, direction, encouragement, and strength when needed. A maieutic leader helps birth the creativity of the group members and rejoices in the success of the whole group. The maieutic leader encourages others to share in leading the group.

To participate in the maieutic process of teaching and learning is to serve as a midwife, that is, to assist in a birthing process of bringing into the light a new creation from within the recesses of another's soul, mind, body, and spirit. The midwife assists the creator to expel from the womb that which has been nurtured, nourished, and warmed into viability. The midwife implants nothing from without and brings only her skill and strength to coach the natural process, albeit a process fraught with danger, labor, and pain.

Scheduling the Disciple Making Process

In one sense it is not entirely accurate to speak about scheduling events in the disciple making process, since a congregation will need to respond to inquirers as they are identified at any point throughout the year. An inquirer may not be ready at first to commit to a weekly gathering with others who are exploring the scriptures, Christian life, and teachings. People who have been exploring the Christian faith for a fairly long amount of time may not be quite ready for baptism or affirmation of baptism, even when others who have spent the same amount of time in preparation are ready. The process is intended to be flexible to each person's timetable and needs. At the same time, much of congregational life and planning is oriented to a calendar, and it is helpful to think about offering key entry points for a disciple making ministry in ways that make sense to your congregation's life and rhythms.

The following are three basic possibilities that may also be adapted to serve the needs of particular congregations, as well as the needs of inquirers and other participants at a given time:

PROGRAMMATIC YEAR PROCESS

The inquiry stage may begin in early fall, toward the end of the season after Pentecost. The next stage of exploration may begin later in the fall, perhaps by late October or early November. The beginning of Lent provides the beginning for the third stage of intense preparation, which culminates in Holy Week with the Three Days (Maundy Thursday, Good Friday, and the Vigil of Easter). Meanwhile, the entire fifty-day season of Easter through the Day of Pentecost provides a time for the fourth stage of reflection on baptismal living.

YEAR-LONG

A year-long process may be similar to the process outlined above, but with opportunities for participants to come into the process earlier and with *several entry points* to the inquiry stage, which can occur several times as needed throughout the year. While candidates for baptism might wish to be baptized at the Vigil of Easter, regardless of when they started the process, another possibility for baptism could be at the Baptism of Our Lord in early January, with the season of Advent providing a period of intense preparation.

A condensed three- to four-month process allows a congregation to offer two times during the year when participants may enter the process. One might begin inquiry in late summer or early fall with baptisms and affirmations celebrated on the Baptism of Our Lord Sunday that occurs in early January. The second opportunity could occur with the inquiry stage beginning no later than Epiphany, with celebration of baptisms and affirmations during the Vigil of Easter.

Launch Guide for Making Disciples

☐ Gather resources. Provide at least one copy of this book, *Go Make Disciples*, for each potential team member, as well as one companion CD-ROM ❂ belonging to the whole team in order to make copies of items intended for individual participants.

☐ Recruit a disciple making team leader and share resources.

☐ Recruit, assemble, and train the remainder of the disciple making team (see Starting a Disciple Making Team, pages 53-57).

☐ Consider visiting a congregation that practices a form of making disciples based on the catechumenate or attend a training event as a team. Contact the North American Association for the Catechumenate (www.catechumenate.org) or denominational leaders who support and train for this work.

☐ Gather the team for prayer. Pray for each other, for your congregation, and for those who might enter the journey with you. Saturate the entire process with prayer.

☐ Provide team members with position descriptions as well as the *Go Make Disciples* resource.

☐ Prepare a timetable and outline for sessions.

☐ Review the worship rites that will be used with participants.

☐ Educate the congregation about making disciples through adult forums, sermons, temple talks, newsletter articles.

- ☐ Publicize disciple making to members, guests, and inquirers. This may include brochures, bulletin inserts, newsletter articles, and notices on your congregation's Web site and social networks.

- ☐ Develop a list of potential inquirers to invite.

- ☐ Make the invitation for inquiry (Come and See) sessions. A face-to-face invitation is more effort but more effective than an e-mail blast. Use the best quality of communication for the specific people you are trying to reach. Be clear about when and where you intend to meet. Make it understood that no one is being asked to commit to join the church or to be baptized at this time. Do not be afraid to invite people who may not be on the list!

- ☐ Pray for the people who will come, especially in the congregation's intercessory prayers for a few weeks leading up to inquiry sessions.

- ☐ Begin to compile a list of potential sponsors for inquirers.

- ☐ Pray for those who will be leaders and sponsors.

Fifty Ways to Involve the Congregation in Making Disciples

AS YOUR CONGREGATION CONSIDERS AND PREPARES FOR ENGAGING IN DISCIPLE MAKING MINISTRY

1. In a sermon or teaching setting imagine walking with an adult to the font. Wonder aloud: "Where would we find an unbaptized adult?" This process works with only one person, even with a baptized seeker.

2. Send a group of three or more to a disciple making (catechumenate) training session. Consult with the North American Association for the Catechumenate (www.catechumenate.org) for current offerings or to organize training in your area.

3. In varied ways inform the congregation of what this ministry is and what it aims to do.

4. Post articles on your church Web site and in e-newsletters about the process of making disciples (see the companion CD-ROM ❄ for specific items).

5. Say it repeatedly: "This is a lay driven ministry! Everyone will have a role to play in it!"

6. Ask the congregation to join in prayer for discernment of whether or not to implement and support this ministry.

7. Prayerfully discern who in the congregation possess the gifts and graces for serving on the disciple making ministry team (see Starting a Disciple Making Team, pages 53-57).

8. Hold an introductory meeting that includes a time for people to indicate their desire or willingness to serve. Welcome all levels of commitment. Notify the whole congregation of the formation of a team and invite people to consider attending the introductory meeting.

9. Decide on the name you will use for the process in your congregation. This resource primarily uses the phrase *making disciples* to describe what many congregations understand to be the *catechumenate*. You may wish to use either one of these ways in communicating your congregation's disciple making process.

Still other congregations opt for names like The Way, Journey, or Search. The name you use is not really all that essential, but the actual process is.

10. Announce the launch of this ministry and give some of the details, including names of the team members and start date and time.

DURING INQUIRY

11. In preaching and other ways, inform the congregation that inquiry is God's work through all people in a congregation, especially in helping to identify who are strangers to the gospel and are being awakened to the nearness of God's reign (Mark 1:15).

12. Pray for those searching for meaning, God, and faith in the intercessory prayers on a regular basis.

13. Help the congregation understand and appreciate that when baptized persons are included in the process their baptism will always be claimed and honored.

14. Actively recruit sponsors with an eye to those who have the gift of faith, wisdom, and hospitality. Choose sponsors carefully so the relationship is a good match.

15. Ask covenant groups, committees, teams, and administrative groups to pray for inquirers.

16. Light a candle in worship each week for those who are inquiring.

17. If there are members who have a powerful story to share of their own seeking, consider inviting them to participate in an inquiry session to tell of their search. (Caution: this is sharing to invite deeper questions, not a way of seeking an immediate response.)

18. In preaching and other formation settings, call the congregation to join the inquirers in discerning God's calling in the arenas of daily life ministry: home, leisure, work, community, wider world, church life and outreach, and spiritual health. For more information go to www.membermission.org.

AT THE RITE OF WELCOME

19. Ask the congregation to turn and face the door when the inquirers and their sponsors approach to enter (if your congregation uses at least a portion of the rite of welcome at the beginning of the service).

20. See that the congregation has an opportunity to commit to pray and help the catechumens and the candidates for affirmation of baptism to know God and to discover the way of following Christ.

21. Have a baptized child or youth present a Bible to each new catechumen or to those seeking to (re)affirm.

22. Urge all to introduce themselves to those welcomed following the rite.

DURING THE EXPLORATION STAGE

23. Share with the congregation that this stage is about hearing the word of God and practicing response in worship, prayer, and reflection on scripture and life, while also enacting God's love and justice in all areas of life.

24. Ask members of the congregation who are engaged in ministries of service to the poor and marginalized to invite the catechumens, affirmers, and their sponsors to participate in the ministry.

25. Urge people to continue to introduce themselves to the catechumens and affirmers so that faces and names become familiar.

AT THE RITE OF ENROLLMENT

26. Ask the congregation for their continuing welcome and support of the candidates in their journey toward the waters of baptism.

27. Invite the congregation to participate actively in the intercessions for those just enrolled; for the conversion of their affections, desires, and commitments; for their sponsors and teachers; their families and friends; for the pastor and people; and for the church, the world, and all in need.

28. Tell the congregation that weekly worship will include prayers for the enrolled.

29. Print the names of candidates and (re)affirmers in the worship leaflet each week and ask the congregation to pray for them by name each day.

30. Provide members with a robust prayer that serves as a model for their daily prayers for the candidates.

31. Call the candidates forward with their sponsors and pray for them during worship with the congregation extending hands toward them or coming to stand with them during the prayers.

32. Dramatize the Lenten (year A) gospel readings from the lectionary with the congregation singing a short repeated response. See Worship Resources in the Bibliography.

33. When the creed is to be presented, ask the congregation to sign a specially printed copy of it in advance. Do the same thing with the printed copy of the Lord's Prayer when it is presented.

34. Remind people that the Vigil of Easter is the central event of the Christian calendar and their presence will give witness to the congregation's welcome and solidarity for the candidates.

35. Plan the Vigil of Easter in ways that call for many people, including children and youth, to participate in celebrating and telling God's story in word and sacraments (see the Bibliography for resources).

AT THE VIGIL OF EASTER AND IN THE WEEKS THAT FOLLOW

36. Ask all to join in applause or other culturally appropriate action when the newly baptized are presented as new sons and daughters of God.

37. Have a signup sheet for hosts to provide festive food and drink for reflection sessions of the newly baptized following baptism.

38. Invite the members of the congregation to host the newly baptized in their homes or at a restaurant for a festive meal.

39. Ask members to invite and welcome the newly baptized and affirmers to be part of their weekly covenant groups, Bible study, or other groups as a means of providing a setting for ongoing support in discipleship and baptismal living.

40. Plan a liturgy of affirmation of vocation on the Day of Pentecost or on another Sunday a few weeks after baptism. Make the day a festival of the work of the Spirit in all of the baptized and invite the newly baptized to speak about specific ministries in the world and the church to which they have discerned a call.

41. If some people say, "Hey! I am jealous. I wish my baptism had been that special!" respond, "Wasn't it great that all of us got to journey with them and make theirs special?" Affirm the communal participation and joy of our one baptism.

42. Do follow up with each of the newly baptized and the affirmers to see how they are doing and to encourage their participation in one of the congregation's ongoing covenant or reflection groups.

ON THE DAY OF PENTECOST
(OR ANOTHER SUNDAY A FEW WEEKS AFTER BAPTISM)

43. Orient the liturgy around the affirmation of ministry in daily life. Involve the congregation in making this festive and reflective.

AFTER THE CYCLE HAS CONCLUDED

44. Invite the congregation to engage in a simple evaluation answering questions like: What went well? What was most meaningful to you? At what point did you most actively participate? How could we do it better next time? Your disciple making team can take these responses into account in planning for next time.

45. Write a story of your congregation's disciple making journey—its highlights and impact on participants, the congregation, the community, and the wider world. Share the good news with the congregation, Web site visitors, your denominational judicatory, and the Web site of the North American Association for the Catechumenate (www.catechumenate.org).

46. Encourage and pray for the ministry of the baptized and their attentiveness to relationships in work, leisure, and other settings. The Holy Spirit is already drawing people to faith; they are looking for an open, welcoming person who represents the gospel.

47. In preaching and other settings have ongoing reflection on baptism and baptismal living. Help all to claim what a difference baptism makes.

48. Plan occasions for all to affirm the baptismal covenant, especially at the Vigil of Easter, the Day of Pentecost, the Baptism of Our Lord, and All Saints Day. Ask the whole congregation the baptismal questions that give concrete shape as to how they intend to live. Then invite them to come and touch the water to remember baptism.

49. Live God's abundance and generosity together in sign and symbol: plenty of water (even a baptismal pool), lots of oil, weekly communion, and many witnesses sent out to love and serve.

50. Make strong use of the baptismal font or pool, especially in the gathering time and the sending forth to baptismal living in which we make our invisible baptismal promises visible.

Inquiry

Snapshot of Inquiry ☯

A time when the church invites all who would listen to come and consider the joyous possibility of living the Christian life. Participants are known as inquirers.

STAGE QUESTIONS: Are you feeling drawn to participate more deeply in the Christian journey of faith? What questions do you have about the faith?

ISSUE: Whether or not to enter into an intentional process of exploring the Christian faith through the guidance and support of a sponsor, a disciple making team, and a congregation.

TIMELINE: This stage may be entered at any time. Its duration is dependent on the inquirer's readiness to move to the next stage, as discerned by the candidate and the community. For those congregations that follow a liturgical year timeline, having the inquiry stage in the fall works well.

PROCESS: This is an open and hospitable time, mostly informal, which allows inquirers to ask questions about the Christian faith, share stories, and come to understand the general outlines of the disciple making process.

TEAM'S AND CONGREGATION'S ROLES: Offering opportunities for gatherings of inquirers to ask questions in order to come to a sense of whether to proceed to the rite of welcome and to the next stage of exploration (usually lengthier). Inquiry may be offered at different times and locations and is led by catechists, small group leaders, and other members of the disciple making team.

Leads to readiness to explore the possibility of baptism and the Christian way of life.

Welcome

Welcome is at the heart of making disciples. The word *welcome* implies there is a meeting between people, an acceptance to be one's self, and a receiving of another with kindness. Also at work, in a word or gesture of welcome, is curiosity and mystery. The present and the future of our time together is both known and unknown. Making disciples embodies welcome through reflection and action, in word and ritual. The first stage of making disciples is simply to create a space for welcome. Welcome happens in many forms and places. Some churches call such an inquiry stage, "Come and See," and have their gatherings in the church. One congregation decided to meet in a pub with the intention to bring in others who might be searching, even purchasing an ad inviting people in the neighborhood to come and see.

There is a sense of welcome when we are called by name. In a liturgical rite of welcome used by many congregations, people are actually called by name and invited to come into God's house in order to be in relationship with God's people and to dwell in the word of God. One of the most moving and profound aspects often included in a rite of welcome is the marking of the cross on different parts of an inquirer's body while proclaiming these words: "Receive the sign of the cross on your ears that you may hear the voice of the Lord, receive the sign of the cross on your lips that you may respond to the word of God, receive the sign of the cross on your shoulders that you may bear the gentle yoke of Christ." In these words and actions, intimacy and vulnerability are intertwined with a deeper sense of belonging.

Welcome happens when the scriptures are broken open and read. As inquirers read and hear God's word, they tell stories, ask questions, and begin forming relationships in a Christian community. In these times acceptance of one another grows as we practice deep listening together. So often in life we are quick to respond to one another with answers and suggestions, but as we listen more deeply to one another there is a unique opportunity to receive one another with compassion and grace, wonder and love. With the notion of welcome, there is the intention to be in relationship with others and to deepen those relationships in the context of a community.

Actions of the Inquiry Stage

- The duration of this stage varies. It could be days, weeks, or possibly even years. It depends on the needs of the seeker.

- In lieu of formal sessions, inquiry may take the form of personal conversations.

- Sessions held are open-ended without a script. They are generally informal and conversational in tone.

- Questions and needs of the inquirers set the agenda.

- Inquirers may be invited to share their life stories or what brought them to a particular faith community.

- Longtime members of the congregation might be invited to share their faith stories.

- Stories from the Bible may be told and discussed.

- The congregation's story may be shared.

- The story of the particular tradition (Episcopal, Lutheran, Presbyterian, Methodist, Reformed, United Church, and so on) could be shared.

- Each inquirer is matched with a particular sponsor.

HELP INQUIRERS CONSIDER:

- Do the stories of the Bible and this particular community bring meaning to my life?

- Do I want to go further with this faith community?

- Do I want to embark on a Christian journey?

- Am I prepared to make a formal commitment to explore the possibility of baptism or affirmation of baptism?

The congregation's posture toward inquirers is always one of welcome and hospitality. Create an open space. Listen to inquirers' questions and stories. God has placed these people in your midst. Let them guide the way.

Gathering Inquirers

Identifying Potential Inquirers

As a congregation plans to engage in the work of making disciples, offer specific invitations to upcoming inquirer sessions with a number of non-members who may already have a connection with the congregation:

- Parents who have recently enrolled their children in Sunday school, vacation Bible school, or other children's programs that the congregation provides.

- People who have returned to church participation after a period of absence.

- People who have been visitors at worship in recent months.

- People who have sought out the church in a time of crisis or specific need.

- People who participate in one or more ministries of the church, such as musical ensembles or educational programs.

- People who attend a concert series or other cultural offerings by the congregation.

- People who attend programs offered by outside organizations using the church's facilities.

- People who are friends or relatives of current members.

Whether it happens during an initial group meeting with other inquirers or even in advance of such a meeting, a disciple making team needs to assess how best to support each individual. Many congregations will identify three basic types of inquirers: adults (or older youth) who may be interested in baptism, adults who have already been baptized but still need instruction and formation in Christian faith prior to affirmation of baptism, and people who are already active in another congregation (or who have recently been) and are interested in transferring their membership. Let us deal with the last type of inquirer first.

RECEIVING ADULT NEWCOMERS BY TRANSFER

Adult newcomers who have recently been active members of another congregation (or perhaps they still are considered as such) may not be interested in or even need an extended process of faith formation. They are simply in need of transferring their membership from another congregation, whether it is of the same denomination, another denomination with which there is a full communion agreement, or another reasonably similar tradition. People who are transferring their membership may simply need to:

- request that a letter of transfer be sent from their previous congregation;

- be introduced to people and customs of the new congregation in a fairly short amount of time;

- be assigned to a companion (or perhaps a companion household if it is more than just one individual being received) for intentional guidance and support during at least the first six months to one year of membership;

- be received as members according to denominational polity; and

- be recognized at a regular worship service of the congregation some Sunday.

RECEIVING ADULT NEWCOMERS BY AFFIRMATION OF BAPTISM

Adult newcomers who have been baptized at some previous time but who have not had much, if any, instruction or formation in Christian practices would likely benefit from a process of faith formation leading to affirmation of baptism (or an equivalent rite in your tradition). This book describes a disciple making process in this and the next three chapters that could be very helpful in guiding someone into mature faith, along with being received by affirmation of baptism. Discipleship development may also be appropriate for people who are already members of a congregation but who wish to experience intentional renewal in their faith followed by (re)affirmation of baptism; thereby not requiring a rite of welcome, but support and encouragement in other ways. Non-member parents who are requesting baptism for their children may benefit from a disciple making process that would include affirmation of baptism for themselves and a rite of welcome that anticipates baptism for their children.

RECEIVING ADULT NEWCOMERS BY BAPTISM

Adult newcomers who have not been baptized would benefit from a process of faith formation leading to baptism. When the church baptizes infants or young children, it expects that they will be formed in faith by parents and sponsors in the years following baptism. When older youth and adults are baptized, instruction in the holy scriptures and formation in the Christian disciplines of prayer, worship, and service happen in anticipation of baptism. This book also describes such a process of supporting older youth and adults who are preparing for baptism.

Scheduling Inquiry Sessions

In many congregations, it is frequently helpful to schedule inquiry sessions at least twice a year: once shortly after the academic year has begun (perhaps late September or early October), and another shortly after the beginning of a new calendar year (mid-January). Very large congregations or those that work with a high number of newcomers may find it useful to have even more inquiry sessions staggered throughout the year. You may find that your congregation's programming is not as much dictated by the academic year as it is by other seasonal factors, and will likely discover other times that may be more appropriate for inquiry sessions in your setting.

Assessing Inquirers' Needs

After you have identified any potential newcomers to your congregation, you will want to publicize plans for upcoming inquiry sessions. It is ordinarily helpful to contact each potential newcomer household personally, even if a blanket invitation has been made to everyone. Ordinarily people do respond better to a phone call or a face-to-face contact.

In speaking directly with potential newcomers you will likely gain some information about what each person's needs might be and how a possible group might break down according to the three basic newcomer types identified above. Even if you may plan to hold a number of inquiry and discipleship sessions together for various categories of people, many teams have discovered that it is beneficial to form separate small groups to address certain needs and backgrounds more specifically. Even if people anticipating baptism and people returning to the church have some of the same needs to understand the scriptures and central church teachings, their unique spiritual histories may identify different pastoral needs. People who are utterly new to the gospel story will likely bring a different set of challenges and questions with them than will those who left the church during adolescence or after a divorce. For this reason it is often desirable to work distinctly with candidates for baptism, returning members who will be candidates for affirmation of baptism, non-member parents requesting baptism for their children, those on journeys of renewal, and people who are already active in church life but are interested in transferring their membership to a new congregation.

If it is not already clear what set of needs any group of inquirers may represent at a given time, the disciple making team should have many more insights after the initial inquiry session, a description of which follows.

Suggested Outline of an Initial Inquiry Session

DAY/TIME: Possibly a Sunday afternoon or evening, though it may be at any time during the week.

DURATION: 60-75 minutes

SETTING: A room with just enough chairs for all attendees that have been set into a circle or semicircle (place chairs into two or more concentric circles if needed because of the size of the group). Tables are not needed—they would only get in the way.

USEFUL ITEMS:

1. Simple refreshments available as people are gathering will provide a welcoming environment, even just one or two beverage options and a tray filled with small pieces of fruit.

2. Provide peel-off name tags and markers for group members to use as they are getting to know one another.

3. Have basic printed information about the congregation (weekly or monthly newsletters and general brochures) available as handouts for inquirers.

AGENDA:

1. The team leader or catechist welcomes inquirers, explains the purpose of the gathering, and introduces members of the team who are present. If the number of inquirers is too small to be divided into small groups later, allow for introductions of inquirers present at this time.

2. A team member leads the group in prayer.

3. The team leader or catechist introduces the storytelling component, which is the chief purpose of the gathering.

4. If there are more than six inquirers, it will probably be helpful to divide into small groups, each having four to six inquirers and a small group leader.

5. Before beginning the storytelling activity, invite all attendees to help themselves to any beverages or other refreshments that are available.

6. If dividing into small groups, the small group leader introduces himself or herself to the group and asks other group members to introduce themselves.

7. Within the small groups (or in the large group if it will not be dividing) use one of the storytelling activities among the pages that follow, or simply ask the question, "How did you come to inquire about the Christian faith here and now?" Allow several minutes for this activity, since it is the main purpose of this initial gathering. Each inquirer and small group leader should have ample opportunity to tell his or her faith story in an unrushed manner, uninterrupted by comments from others in the group. Provide each group member with an equal amount of time to speak.

8. Following the telling of all stories, the small group leader thanks group members for their sharing and concludes the group time with prayer.

9. Prior to dismissal, exchange contact information among inquirers and respective small group leaders and inform inquirers about the meeting times and places for upcoming sessions.

Storytelling

My Life Story ◑

Growing in the understanding of faith involves recognizing how God has been a part of our lives in the past. While we can pinpoint important events in our lives, we don't always recognize God's activity in the turns and twists our lives take. We read Bible stories about God's involvement with humanity from creation through the establishment of the Christian church, and we are able to see how people of faith have recognized their place in the salvation story God enacts for the world. God continues to unfold the promises told in the Bible and made known in Jesus, the Word made flesh. All creation has a place in the salvation story of God's grace.

ITEMS NEEDED

Participants will need paper and markers for this exercise. Long lengths of paper (large sheets of newsprint or rolls of paper) are useful.

ACTIVITY DESCRIPTION

This activity invites participants to make timelines of their lives. The catechist may provide a model timeline with categories or topics for participants to consider in telling their stories.

INSTRUCTIONS

- Beginning on the left of the paper, the timeline is chronologically ordered by year.

- The individual may begin by noting his or her birth date and naming parents, older siblings, and other significant family members.

- The timeline ends on the right side of the paper with an arrow pointing into the future.

- Each person marks significant events, relationships, places, insights, achievements and so forth on the timeline as they are recalled.

- Additional notes may be added to the timeline as awareness of God's part in one's life grows.

- Participants may add comments about key values held at various points in life. The person's changing image of God could be another set of notations.

- The timeline may be saved and referred to again and again in prayer, reflection, and discussion. The individual may choose to share some or all of the timeline in a group gathering or in private conversation with a sponsor. This personal history provides a valuable tool for an individual to reflect on how his or her life has unfolded and to consider how God has been present in the unfolding of that life.

- Consider these when forming your life's timeline: family, events, church, images of God, education, relationships, places, values.

My Story ◉

The following categories, phrases, and questions are prompts that you might use to tell your life story. Consider the possibilities on this page only as guides to help you get started. They are not intended to be exhaustive or to limit you in any way.

ETHNIC HERITAGE
Stories our elders have told us about their lives and those before them

RELATIONAL
Who we are in relationship to other people: son/daughter/brother/sister/aunt/uncle/cousin/niece/nephew/mother/father, etc.

OCCUPATIONAL/VOCATIONAL
- Butcher, baker, candlestick maker
- Gardener, care-giver, traveler
- Neighbor, friend, advocate

PSYCHOLOGICAL
- The environment in which we were raised (loving, abusive, consistent, inconsistent)
- The environment in which we have lived/are currently living (loving, abusive, consistent, inconsistent)

EXPERIENCES

- Joys and tragedies of our lives; the ups and downs
- The outstanding opportunities
- The unbearable sorrows
- All the things, big and small, that have shaped us and formed us into the people we are today

FAITH STORIES

- What is your conversion story (a moment in time or movement through time)?
- How has your faith changed?
- What are the mysteries?
- Identify the desert sojourns and the prodigal returns.

WHAT IS YOUR GROWING EDGE?

- Where are you challenged today?
- To what are you being called or drawn?

Identifying Sponsors

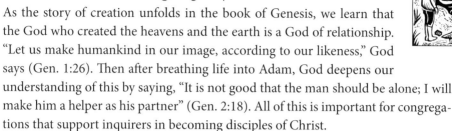

As the story of creation unfolds in the book of Genesis, we learn that the God who created the heavens and the earth is a God of relationship. "Let us make humankind in our image, according to our likeness," God says (Gen. 1:26). Then after breathing life into Adam, God deepens our understanding of this by saying, "It is not good that the man should be alone; I will make him a helper as his partner" (Gen. 2:18). All of this is important for congregations that support inquirers in becoming disciples of Christ.

Just as with life itself, the disciple making process is built on relationships. As we create space for inquirers to develop relationships of trust with one another, we also see the goodness in identifying helpers from the community who will journey with them as partners. These partners, or sponsors, are people who embody the love of God and the welcome of the whole community for each inquirer. They are not teachers or mentors, but pilgrims joining pilgrims on a path to spiritual renewal.

The primary advantage that sponsors have is that they are familiar with the physical and relational space into which the inquirers are walking. Sponsors are active members of the congregation who already know the lay of the land. They know the patterns of worship and the paths of service that shape congregational life. They know many of the other people who gather each week, and they bear within themselves many of the sacred stories that reflect the unique character of their spiritual home. With all of this, they are graciously equipped to help inquirers feel at home in a new environment and to come to know the people and practices of the congregation more fully.

How to Choose Appropriate Sponsors

No set prescription exists for choosing a sponsor for each inquirer. Some common patterns are emerging, however, and they may be helpful for those who are looking for a place to begin.

- First, sponsors and participants are usually people of the same gender. Though not a hard and fast rule, the practice seems to work well in most circumstances.

- Second, sponsors and participants often have some areas where their interests and their life circumstances naturally connect.

- Third, good sponsors are good listeners. They may be outgoing and talkative or quiet and reflective, but they know how to be attentive to the words and the insights of a participant.

- Fourth, good sponsors are people who are seeking spiritual growth and renewal themselves. They don't pretend to have all the answers or to have arrived at some higher level of spiritual maturity. Instead, they see the invitation to be a sponsor as an invitation to learn and grow with others.

- Fifth, good sponsors are good advocates. They learn about the gifts and interests of inquirers and they help them find ways to connect those with ministry in daily life. They introduce inquirers to new people each week and they stay in touch with them beyond Sunday mornings.

- Sixth, good sponsors are committed to worshiping and attending disciple making sessions with an inquirer each week.

- Finally, good sponsors are trustworthy. They can be expected to keep sensitive information that they find out about a participant in confidence. Nothing destroys a relationship more than a person who talks about someone else behind the other person's back.

Many would say that the best way to start the process of identifying sponsors is to develop a compelling position description that lifts up qualities such as the ones mentioned above. When the position of sponsor is included in the congregation's list of service opportunities, people can discern whether this is something to which God may be calling them. Of course many people will only come forward if they are asked, so it is also important to look for people who possess the desired gifts and then approach them with a personal invitation to serve as a sponsor.

Though it does not always work out this way, frequently an inquirer who has entered the life of the congregation has been introduced to it by a member who would make an ideal sponsor. When such a relationship already exists with an inquirer, it would be good to explore if the potential sponsor in question could fulfill the expectations identified above.

Suggested Outline of Subsequent Inquiry Sessions

DAY/TIME: Possibly a Sunday afternoon or evening, though it may be at any time during the week.

DURATION: 60-75 minutes

SETTING: A room with just enough chairs for all attendees that have been set into a circle or semicircle (place chairs into two or more concentric circles if needed because of the size of the group). Tables are not needed—they would only get in the way.

USEFUL ITEMS:
1. Simple refreshments available as people are gathering will provide a welcoming environment, even just one or two beverage options and a tray filled with small pieces of fruit.

2. Provide peel-off name tags and markers for group members to use if they are still getting to know one another.

3. Have basic printed information about the congregation (weekly or monthly newsletters and general brochures) available as handouts for inquirers.

4. A Bible for each participant or a printout of the scripture reading to be used for reflection.

AGENDA:
1. The team leader or catechist welcomes inquirers (with their sponsors if inquirer/sponsor matches have already been made), explains the purpose of the gathering, and introduces members of the team who are present. If the number of inquirers is too small to be divided into small groups later, allow for introductions of inquirers at this time.

2. A team member leads the group in prayer.

3. A catechist may use a brief amount of time (15-20 minutes) to present a topic to the group. The topic could be related to a question that one or more inquirers have already asked. (A number of inquirer questions might begin: "What

does your church believe about _____?") Speaking about one or two significant ministries of the congregation that involve a fairly large number of people could also be a way of continuing the storytelling that began with the initial inquiry session.

4. If there are more than six inquirers, it will probably be helpful to divide into small groups, each having four to six inquirers and a small group leader.

5. Before beginning the scripture reflection, invite all attendees to help themselves to any beverages or other refreshments that are available.

6. If dividing into small groups with group members who have not met before, the small group leader introduces himself or herself to the group and asks other group members to introduce themselves.

7. Within the small groups (or in the large group if it will not be dividing) reflect on a scripture passage. It could be a passage in which people hear and respond to the call of God in their lives (such as John 1:35-42), a passage that will be used in worship the preceding or following Sunday, or any other passage that is considered to be appropriate to the needs of the group. Consider using one of the outlines provided in the Scripture Reflection Methods section (pages 140-143). Allow several minutes for this activity and provide an opportunity for all group members to speak.

8. Following the scripture reflection, the small group leader thanks group members for their sharing and concludes the group time with prayer.

9. Prior to dismissal, exchange contact information among new inquirers and respective small group leaders and inform inquirers about the meeting times and places for upcoming sessions.

This basic outline may be repeated as many times as necessary during the inquiry stage.

Preparation for the Rite of Welcome

The following is a suggested format to use in preparing inquirers and members of the team for a rite of welcome. Many congregations use similar rites of welcome for those who are already baptized and for those who are preparing for affirmation of baptism, though there are some important distinctions. Those who are preparing for affirmation are acknowledged as baptized members of the church who may already be communing. While many of the instructional and formational needs can be similar among both baptized and unbaptized inquirers, baptism is an indelible and distinguishable mark that is recognized in the process of making disciples.

Suggested Agenda

5:00–5:40 pm	Meal
5:40–5:50 pm	Large Group—Setting the Context
5:50–6:30 pm	Small Groups—Reflection Questions
6:30–6:50 pm	Rehearsal for Rite of Welcome (with team members and sponsors only)

LARGE GROUP

During the large group presentation, a leader sets the context for the evening's discussion in these or similar words.

You will each have an opportunity to be welcomed in a formal way to this congregation. This formal welcoming is called the rite of welcome. You are invited to take part in it if and when you feel you are ready to take the next step of exploring Christian faith with the guidance and support of this congregation. The rite of welcome takes place on a Sunday morning during a regular worship service. Your sponsor will stand with you as you are invited to journey more deeply into a life of faith.

Many things take place during the rite of welcome (customize this according to the particular order in use by your denomination and congregation):

- The inquirers will appear before the congregation (perhaps even at the entrance to the worship space) and will be presented by their sponsors.

- The presiding minister will ask what inquirers seek from God's church. Inquirers may respond in a variety of ways (indicate some possibilities during this time according to the particular rite that your congregation uses).

- The presiding minister will ask if each inquirer will be faithful in hearing the word of God and following Christ. The inquirer responds affirmatively.

- The congregation will pledge its support to the inquirers.

- A sponsor will make the sign of the cross on inquirers' foreheads, possibly also signing the senses, the shoulders, the hands, and the feet.

- A Bible may be presented to the inquirers.

- A presiding minister will lead a prayer for the inquirers.

- The inquirers will usually return to their places with the rest of the worshipers at this time.

SMALL GROUP REFLECTION

- Have you ever worn a cross or a symbol of faith? (Why or why not?)

- Are there any symbols of faith visible in your home?

- Take a moment to think about and visualize the cross being made on your body by another person, or sponsors making the cross on another person. What do you think it means to bear the cross of Christ or to take on Christ? What do you think this experience will mean for you?

- The crosses traced on your body will be invisible to others. How might it be made visible to others?

REHEARSAL

Usually it will be helpful for the team (team leader, small group leaders, sponsors, liturgist, and possibly the presiding minister) to rehearse most of the rite together in advance. Participants usually do not attend rehearsals themselves, since rehearsing these moments in advance dulls the full impact of the actual rite; furthermore, if sponsors have carefully rehearsed the rites they will be able to guide participants. Be sure to explain at what point in the service the rite of welcome will take place and what inquirers will be expected to say or do for themselves. If there is to be a reception in honor of the inquirers after the service, inform the team.

CLOSING PRAYER

Lord Jesus, you bore the cross to take away the sin of the world. Give us strength and courage to bear your cross so that we might be witnesses of your love to all the world. Amen.

Exploration

Snapshot of Exploration ✷

A time when the church welcomes inquirers to share in its central
Christian practices and they enter into an open-ended period
of apprenticeship and formation in worship, prayer, reflection
on scripture, and ministries of service and justice to others in
need. Unbaptized participants are often known as catechumens.
Participants expecting to affirm or reaffirm baptism may be called
affirmers, reaffirmers, or (re)affirmation candidates.

STAGE QUESTION: Are you ready to be baptized and share your life with the
church for the life of the world?

ISSUE: Testing the depth and perseverance of exploring life as a Christian.

TIMELINE: Exploration is open-ended and may be entered at any time. Its duration
is dependent on the candidate's readiness to move to the next stage, as discerned by
the candidate and the community.

PROCESS: Public participation in hearing and responding to the word of God
in worship; being a part of weekly sessions with catechists and a group leader for
instruction, formation, scriptural reflection, prayer, and the discovery of various
Christian practices, especially through service ministries.

SPONSOR'S AND CONGREGATION'S ROLES: Coaching the catechumens in
the discernment of readiness for baptism. Accompanying affirmation candidates as
they deepen their life in Christ.

Leads to a commitment to be prepared for baptism or
affirmation of baptism on a specific day.

Reflection on the Rite of Welcome

During the first session following the rite of welcome (perhaps even later on the same day), allow catechumens, (re)affirmers, and sponsors time to reflect on their experience of the rite.

Some possible questions:

- How did you experience the rite?

- Were you surprised by anything?

- Were you confused by anything?

- Is there anything that you wish could be explained?

Exploration

"Listen with the ear of your heart." These words, from the prologue in the *Rule of St. Benedict*, resonate with the heart and soul of the disciple making process. The word *catechumen* means "sound in the ear." Thus, a disciple is invited to listen to God's word and so learn and embrace the Christian life. Imagine a process shaped by the admonition to listen with the ear of the heart. How might this core value shape our catechesis? How might we invite seekers into a deeper engagement with God? How can they engage in deep listening?

When imagining how best to facilitate catechetical sessions, it is important to ask the questions above. There is not just one method to use in faith formation. Consider a variety of ways to help those in the disciple making process listen and pay attention to scripture, worship, prayer, ministry, and service. Invite them to reflect on their experience and so discover the living God.

Actions of the Exploration Stage

- In this stage, those who were inquirers into the Christian life are encouraged to go deeper.

- Sponsors begin attending sessions with their inquirers. A few icebreakers may be appropriate as the group expands.

- Encourage sponsors to come to each session throughout the process along with the catechumens and the (re)affirmation candidates.

- During each catechetical session focus on readings either from the previous Sunday or those for the upcoming Sunday, making links between the scripture readings and experiences in daily life.

- Allow the themes of the lectionary readings to determine the topics to be discussed in either small or large group settings.

- Consider catechesis on a variety of topics: church history, theology, worship practices, the baptismal covenant, the Ten Commandments, prayer, the creeds, the liturgical year, and the catechisms of the church.

- A single catechist or another team member may lead the teaching.

- Invite people to reflect upon what they hear or have experienced. Stress interactive and reflective teaching.

- Invite reflection on service projects and other areas of ministry within and beyond the congregation (food bank, homeless shelter, mission trip, visiting the homebound, and so forth). Ask: "What did you see? What did you hear? What does this experience say to you about God, Jesus, or the Christian life?"

- Reflect frequently on experiences at worship.

- Bookend disciple making gatherings with prayer. Create a physical environment that is warm, inviting, and sacred. Place chairs in a circle so group members may interact easily with one another (avoid the use of tables). Use an icon or candles to serve as a focal point for prayer and other acts of worship. Use collects, psalms, intercessory prayer, or some form of daily prayer, hymnody, or the repetitive chants of Taizé. These are good ways to center participants or send them off in peace.

- Near the end of this stage let catechumens know that they will be asked to discern whether or not they are ready for baptism.

Carefully planned sessions that are prayerful and inviting will help this time of exploration be a time of listening. Help the catechumens ponder what difference being a Christian makes.

Suggested Outline of Weekly Exploration Sessions

DAY/TIME: Possibly a Sunday morning session, later on Sunday, or another time during the week (preferably as early in the week as possible in order to reflect on Sunday worship).

DURATION: 75-90 minutes

SETTING: A room with just enough chairs for all attendees that have been set into a circle or semicircle (place chairs into two or more concentric circles if needed because of the size of the group). Tables are not needed—they would only get in the way.

USEFUL ITEMS:

1. Light refreshments.

2. A Bible for each participant or a printout of the scripture reading to be used for reflection (if participants received Bibles from the congregation they could be encouraged to bring them to the weekly sessions).

3. Books of worship, prayer books, hymnals, catechisms, or other materials used as devotional or teaching resources.

4. Calendars or other lists containing lectionary (scripture) citations for each week.

5. Copies of bulletins or other worship resources used for the week.

AGENDA:

1. The team leader or catechist welcomes participants along with their sponsors.

2. A team member leads the group in prayer.

3. A catechist may use a brief amount of time (15-20 minutes) to present a topic to the group. The topic could be related to a question that one or more catechumens have already asked, or a topic from the following section (Topics for Groups in the Exploration Stage) could be considered.

4. Divide into small groups if necessary (multiple groups will likely be necessary if there are more than five or six catechumen/sponsor pairs). It will ordinarily be helpful to have separate groups of those preparing for baptism and for affirmation of baptism, simply to respect the baptismal identity and different needs of those who are affirming baptism.

5. Groups that meet on Sunday may reflect on one or more of the readings heard in worship that day. Groups meeting on other days of the week might focus on one or more readings from the upcoming Sunday. Use some form of scripture reflection (see various possibilities in the Scripture Reflection Methods section, pages 140-143).

6. Groups conclude their time with prayers for one another.

This basic outline may be repeated as many times as necessary during the exploration stage.

Topics for Groups in the Exploration Stage

In addition to biblical reflection and prayer, the disciple making groups may include discussion of one or more topics in each session. Topics may range from various doctrinal issues to aspects of worship, the sacraments, and the daily life of a Christian. Topics may be ordered for their relationship to the lectionary for a given week or season. Topics may best be presented in the form of a dialogue or conversation, rather than a purely lecture format. Be aware that each group has different needs and interests, and that what might have been useful for a previous group may be less helpful for a subsequent one.

POSSIBLE TOPICS MAY INCLUDE:

- Sin

- The Trinity (particularly as expressed in one or more creeds of the church)

- Grace

- Word

- Sacraments

- The Ten Commandments

- Prayer—devotional and corporate intercessory prayer

- Worship

- Ministry in daily life

- Mission

- Church history (an overview)

- Denominational history (particularly of one's own denomination)

Other topics may be suggested by catechisms or primary teaching and doctrinal resources in various denominational traditions.

Intercessory Prayer for Disciple Making Groups

In a small group it may be helpful to use the interactive prayer pattern many congregations use in Sunday worship. Encourage individuals to name concerns, thanksgivings, laments, and intercessions. Allow for a short silence for reflective prayer, and then invite all to join in a communal prayer response:

> *Leader:* Lord, in your mercy,
> *Group:* **hear our prayer.**

> *or*
> *Leader:* Hear us, O God.
> *Group:* **Your mercy is great.**

> *or*
> *After each petition, the group could sing a simple Taizé refrain:*
> O Lord, hear my prayer.

> *or*
> *After each petition, sing the repeated refrain:*
> Lord, listen to your children praying.

This is a way to voice individual concerns as well as community and world needs in prayer in a spontaneous fashion. Intercessory prayers may offer up the real concerns of our lives in the present moment.

Another form of intercessory prayer has group members standing or sitting in a circle, with each person praying for the person on his or her right. In this manner every person develops a basic facility for prayer and each person has at least some of his or her concerns acknowledged each week.

Additional prayer possibilities are provided in the Small Group Blessings and Prayers section (pages 149-155).

Discernment for Baptism

Readiness for baptism is a matter that must be determined by every catechumen in combination with leaders on the disciple making team. Individual readiness and the support of a sponsor are the two primary factors to consider. Under-standing the Christian story, growing in faith, and practicing spiri-tual disciplines are additional factors that may be measured quantifi-ably in some way. This is not to say that each catechumen must pass a battery of tests and requirements like a student might need to do in order to earn an academic degree.

Much discernment regarding readiness for baptism might occur rather naturally within the disciple making process. Has a catechu-men been regular in attending worship and disciple making sessions? Has the catechumen been developing a Christian identity? Does the catechumen know key biblical stories and feel comfortable with primary Christian teachings and practices? Has the catechumen pursued one or more forms of minis-try and service to the larger community and world beyond? If a catechumen, her or his sponsor, small group leader, and other members of the disciple making team can answer these questions affirmatively, then a catechumen has likely demonstrated readiness for baptism and might be enrolled for baptism in the near future. If a cat-echumen is still developing a number of these traits though, readiness for baptism may still be a ways off.

While participation in a group with other catechumens may demonstrate some readiness for baptism, mere participation and attendance in group activities do not by themselves determine whether a catechumen's faith development has matured sufficiently. While it is certainly understandable for a catechumen to have questions and even to express some doubts about a number of Christian beliefs and practices, a catechumen needs to express the desire to follow Christ as fully as possible and to give evidence of already having matured in faith. While having a willingness to par-ticipate intentionally in a process of becoming a disciple of Christ is all that might be required prior to the rite of welcome, catechumens who are enrolled for baptism ordinarily have demonstrated significant growth in faith.

Preparation and Rehearsal for the Rite of Enrollment

The following is a suggested format to use in preparing catechumens and members of the disciple making team to participate in a rite of enrollment for baptism, often held on the first Sunday in Lent. Candidates who participate in the rite of enrollment are catechumens who have already discerned readiness for baptism itself (see the previous section on Discernment for Baptism).

One of the regularly scheduled exploration sessions shortly before the rite of enrollment may prepare participants for the rite of enrollment, or the rite of enrollment preparation session might occur separately from the usual exploration sessions.

Note: In some traditions candidates for (re)affirmation may participate in a separate rite of renewal at the beginning of Lent, possibly on Ash Wednesday. Because candidates for (re)affirmation are already baptized, they are not enrolled for baptism. If there is to be a time of public acknowledgment during congregational worship with candidates for (re)affirmation, then they will also need special preparation for their participation in that rite, along with members of the team.

LARGE GROUP

- During the large group presentation a catechist speaks about the role that the rite of enrollment plays in marking the final weeks of preparation for baptism.

- If baptism will take place during the Vigil of Easter, the catechist may speak further about Lent's original focus as a time of preparation for baptism. These days congregations often invite everyone to support baptismal candidates during Lent.

- Inform baptismal candidates and the disciple making team about the date and time when the rite of enrollment will take place (customarily on the first Sunday in Lent).

- Explain that the following elements may take place during the rite of enrollment (customize this according to the particular order in use by your denomination and congregation):

    * Catechists, sponsors, or other representatives of the congregation present baptismal candidates within a regular service of worship.

* The presiding minister asks candidates if they desire to be baptized.

* The presiding minister asks sponsors if candidates have been nurtured by the word of God.

* The congregation pledges its support to the baptismal candidates.

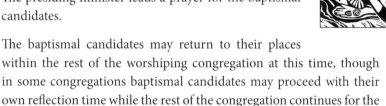

* A sponsor or catechist writes the name of each person to be baptized in the congregation's baptismal register or enrollment book.

* The presiding minister leads a prayer for the baptismal candidates.

* The baptismal candidates may return to their places within the rest of the worshiping congregation at this time, though in some congregations baptismal candidates may proceed with their own reflection time while the rest of the congregation continues for the remainder of the eucharistic liturgy.

REHEARSAL

Usually it will be helpful for the disciple making team (team leader, small group leaders, catechists, sponsors, liturgist, and possibly the presiding minister) to rehearse most of the rite together in advance. In many congregations candidates for baptism do not attend rehearsals themselves, since rehearsing these moments in advance dulls the full impact of the rite; furthermore, if sponsors have carefully rehearsed the rites they will be able to guide baptismal candidates. Be sure to explain at what point in the service the rite of enrollment will take place and what candidates will be expected to say or do for themselves.

CLOSING PRAYER

O Lord, look with love on all who have been marked with the sign of the cross. Lead them through the waters of baptism and raise them up to new life with you, that they may sing your praise through your Son, Jesus Christ our Lord.

SMALL GROUP REFLECTION

- What is the power of a name?

- How do biblical stories demonstrate God's use of names in order to call people to new identities?

- What new identity is emerging in you as you prepare for baptism?

ADDITIONAL PREPARATIONS OF THE DISCIPLE MAKING TEAM
PRIOR TO THE RITE OF ENROLLMENT

- In advance of the rite, ask each baptismal candidate to provide the spelling of her or his name as it should appear in church records. Provide these names to administrative staff of the congregation as well as to sponsors.

- If the congregation does not already have a book of enrollment or baptismal register that may be used for this rite, purchase or make a large, beautiful blank book to be used in the rite.

- Prior to the service, rehearse any sung responses of the rite of enrollment with the congregation.

- Assuage any worries that candidates might have about needing to speak in public or do anything alone.

- In subsequent catechetical sessions, allow candidates and sponsors time to reflect on their experience of the rite.

Go Make Disciples

Intense Preparation

Snapshot of Intense Preparation ●

A time when the church supports candidates for a brief period prior to baptism, often during the season of Lent. While candidates for (re)affirmation are not enrolled (they are already baptized), they nonetheless may reflect more deeply on their own spiritual growth as they anticipate affirmation of baptism soon.

STAGE QUESTIONS: The questions asked at baptism: Do you renounce Satan and all the forces that defy God? Do you confess Jesus Christ . . . and promise to follow him?

ISSUE: Readiness to renounce self-centeredness and evil and to commit to Christ and his direction in daily life.

TIMELINE: This period usually lasts six weeks. Ordinarily it begins on the first Sunday in Lent and culminates with the Vigil of Easter.

PROCESS: Conversion. Candidates bring all of their attitudes, wounds, yearnings, and commitments into the light of Christ.

FOCUS: Encountering Jesus and accepting his call to belong to the reign of God.

SPONSOR'S AND CONGREGATION'S ROLES: Standing with and praying for the candidates in the light of Christ; being transparent about our own need for continual conversion.

Leads to dying and rising with Christ and onward to life with the church as a water-washed, Spirit-born, table-sharing, missional people.

Reflection on the Rite of Enrollment

During the first session following the rite of enrollment (perhaps even later on the same day), allow baptismal candidates and sponsors time to reflect on their experience of the rite.

Some possible questions:

• How did you experience the rite?

• Were you surprised by anything?

• Were you confused by anything?

• Is there anything that you wish could be explained?

Intense Preparation

- A large commitment looms as participants anticipate baptism or affirmation of baptism in the coming weeks. Be aware of the variety of emotions this may evoke and make room to address them as needed.

- This stage usually takes place in Lent, a season when the church focuses on preparation of baptismal candidates and the continual process of conversion for everyone. If baptism or the affirmation of baptism is scheduled for the festival of the Baptism of Our Lord in early January, then the start of the intensive preparation stage may coincide with the beginning of Advent.

- Catechesis during this time anticipates the baptismal liturgy. Sunday gospel readings (particularly during year A of Lent) present themes of repentance, growth in faith, and turning to Christ. Prayers provided in the Blessing of Candidates rites during this period (see the Lutheran Renewing Worship rites on the companion CD-ROM ❂) lift out the themes of baptism and conversion present in all three years of the Lenten lectionary readings. If baptism is to occur during the season of Advent, the anticipation of the coming reign of God and John the Baptist's proclamation about Jesus' baptism with fire and the Holy Spirit provide a good foundation to speak about the experience of conversion. Moreover, the themes of darkness and light that are also present in scripture readings and in other liturgical symbolism of the Advent, Christmas, and Epiphany seasons can be used in ways that echo the Vigil of Easter as well as the centrality of the paschal (Easter) candle in the baptismal liturgy.

- Regardless of the methods that are used or the season in which preparation for baptism occurs, the heart of this stage of intense preparation for baptism is all about the death and resurrection of Christ (also called the *paschal mystery*). Baptism joins each Christian to the death and resurrection of Christ. As Christians recall the gifts of baptism each day, they are encouraged to see daily repentance and renewal as dying to sin and living to God's saving and transformative love in their lives.

- Throughout the season of Lent, or at other times when congregations anticipate baptism and affirmation of baptism, praying for candidates in prior weeks is a way of providing support to them. Alert candidates about these prayers of support from the congregation and encourage their continued commitment to be present at regular worship services.

- Assuage any worries that baptism and affirmation candidates might have about speaking in public or doing anything alone.

Go Make Disciples

Baptismal Preparation

- In the weeks prior to baptism, contact people in your congregation who are responsible for baptismal supplies to let them know how many baptisms there will be so that adequate numbers of towels, gowns, and candles are available.

- Set up a meeting with the sponsors alone just before baptism to rehearse the service.

- Together with the group that is responsible for worship planning in your congregation, consider how the worship space might be arranged in order to make it more conducive to the needs of the baptismal liturgy. Is there sufficient space for the number of baptismal candidates, sponsors, team members, relatives, and other members of the congregation to gather around the font? What is possible in your particular space to enhance the notion of the assembly gathering together around the baptized? If an existing baptismal font is not able to accommodate full immersion or pouring a significant amount of water on baptismal candidates, might a temporary font be constructed for the occasion (see the section on Constructing a Temporary Font, page 173)?

- During a meeting shortly before the baptismal service, speak with candidates for baptism about the possible need to bring special clothes for the baptism itself as well as dry clothes to change into following the baptism. Candidates also need to know how the baptismal water, oil of anointing, and laying on of hands could affect hair styles and makeup. Speak with candidates about what time to come for the service, and advise them that the service might be significantly longer than usual (particularly if it is the Vigil of Easter). Let candidates and their sponsors also know about any reception that may follow the service.

- Fill out certificates ahead of time for the baptismal candidates as well as for sponsors (if that is your congregation's custom).

- Arrange for a festive reception following the baptismal service.

- If a significant number of people will be baptized (particularly if your congregation has not often had adult baptisms in the past), be sure to inform the congregation about what will be happening so that they may plan to attend.

Ideas for Lent and the Three Days

Lent is often used as the time to prepare candidates for baptism or for affirmation of baptism and the Vigil of Easter. Besides the public worship rites that occur during this pivotal time, how might congregations accompany candidates in their journey? How might the ministry of accompanying candidates for baptism and affirmation of baptism be in the forefront of Lenten and Easter celebrations?

IDEAS FOR LENT

- When the rite of enrollment for those who will be baptized takes place on or near the first Sunday in Lent, the book of enrollment (in which those preparing for baptism signed their names) could be prominently displayed somewhere in the worship space throughout the entire season, perhaps near the baptismal font if space allows.

- Include candidates for baptism or affirmation of baptism in the prayers of intercession each week. Encourage the entire congregation to pray for the candidates each day during Lent.

- Speak about how practicing the disciplines of Lent (prayer, fasting, and works of love) is how the whole church accompanies baptismal candidates as they consciously enter more deeply into these Christian practices.

- Choose hymns and other music appropriate to the themes of conversion that are in the lectionary readings for Lent.

- For congregations holding midweek services of prayer, consider designing them around themes of conversion, discipleship, and rebirth.

- Choose a statement of faith as the focus of small group parish gatherings or classes. Consider using catechism materials from your own tradition, or perhaps even materials from another denominational tradition with which your congregation has a relationship (either a full communion agreement or a common support of service ministries in the wider community). Focus on the Apostles' Creed or the Lord's Prayer, since these elements of the liturgy are often handed over to candidates in the weeks prior to baptism.

- Incorporate the journey to baptism in preaching. Sermons that reflect upon the liturgical rite of enrollment for baptismal candidates, a call to renewal or to continuing conversion for (re)affirmers, or the various Lenten blessings serve to draw out the richness and meaning of these journeys for the entire worshiping assembly.

IDEAS FOR HOLY WEEK AND THE THREE DAYS

- If your congregation holds services of daily prayer or holy communion on Monday, Tuesday, and Wednesday in Holy Week, continue to pray for those preparing for baptism or affirmation of baptism.

- Invite candidates for baptism or affirmation of baptism to wash feet on Maundy Thursday.

- Hold a retreat for baptism and affirmation of baptism candidates along with their sponsors to prepare them for the Three Days, or hold one afterward so they may reflect on their experience. Consider similar retreats for the entire congregation.

Suggested Outline of Weekly Sessions during the Stage of Intense Preparation

DAY/TIME: Possibly a Sunday morning session, later on Sunday, or another time during the week (preferably as early in the week as possible in order to reflect on Sunday worship).

DURATION: 75-90 minutes

SETTING: A room with just enough chairs for all attendees that have been set into a circle or semicircle (place chairs into two or more concentric circles if needed because of the size of the group). Tables are not needed—they would only get in the way.

USEFUL ITEMS:

1. Light refreshments.

2. A Bible for each participant or a printout of the scripture reading to be used for reflection.

3. Books of worship, prayer books, hymnals, catechisms, or other materials used as devotional or teaching resources.

4. Calendars or other lists containing lectionary (scripture) citations for each week.

5. Copies of bulletins or other worship resources used for the week.

AGENDA:

1. The team leader or catechist welcomes candidates for baptism and affirmation of baptism along with their sponsors.

2. A team member leads the group in prayer.

3. A catechist may use a brief amount of time (15-20 minutes) to present a topic to the group. The topic could be related to a question that one or more candidates have already asked. Especially as the stage of intense preparation progresses, the topic may be related to the presentations of the Apostles' Creed (third Sunday in Lent) or the Lord's Prayer (fifth Sunday in Lent) that often occur during

these weeks. Other topics integral to this time could be an introduction to the season of Lent, the disciplines of Lent, the baptismal covenant or vows, and preparation for the services of baptism or affirmation of baptism.

4. Divide into small groups if necessary (multiple groups will likely be necessary if there are more than five or six participant/sponsor pairs). It will ordinarily be helpful to have separate groups of those preparing for baptism and for affirmation of baptism, simply to respect the baptismal identity and different needs of those who are affirming baptism.

5. Groups that meet on Sunday may reflect on one or more of the readings heard in worship that day. Groups meeting on other days of the week might focus on one or more readings from the upcoming Sunday. Use some form of scripture reflection (see various possibilities in the Scripture Reflection Methods section, pages 140-143).

6. Groups conclude their time with prayers for one another.

This basic outline may be repeated throughout the intense preparation stage.

Additional Suggestions for Sessions during the Stage of Intense Preparation

Use Year A Lectionary Readings

Especially for congregations having a significant group of baptismal candidates during the season of Lent, consider using the scripture readings from year A of the lectionary, regardless of the actual three-year lectionary cycle currently in use. The gospel readings about Nicodemus (John 3, the second Sunday in Lent of year A), the woman from Samaria (John 4, the third Sunday in Lent of year A), the healing of the man born blind (John 9, the fourth Sunday in Lent of year A) and the raising of Lazarus (John 11, the fifth Sunday in Lent of year A) are powerful stories about conversion and lend themselves particularly well to preparing for baptism.

Reflect on Public Rites of Blessing

As a way of supporting baptismal candidates during their final weeks of preparation, congregations often pray publicly for them on Sundays and during other regularly scheduled worship services during Lent, particularly when baptism will take place at the Vigil of Easter. While the candidates may simply be named in the intercessory prayers of the congregation, a more visible way of highlighting baptismal candidates' journeys is through specific blessings on the third, fourth, and fifth Sundays in Lent. Traditionally the prayers have supported candidates in the work of renouncing evil in their lives.

Reflect on the public occasions of blessing with the baptismal candidates, perhaps by using the following questions:

- Are you strengthened by the prayers of the congregation in these days of preparation?

- How are you guided by God's spirit to resist evil in the world?

- What resources best support you in following God's direction in your life?

Reflect on Presentations

Along with blessing candidates for baptism during Lent, many denominational orders of worship have adopted the practice of presenting (or *handing over*) central texts of the Apostles' Creed and the Lord's Prayer in the weeks preceding baptism (if during Lent, the Apostles' Creed may be presented on the third Sunday in Lent and the Lord's Prayer may be presented on the fifth Sunday in Lent). If your congregation presents these central texts that form the basis for much of Christian faith and practice in the weeks leading up to baptism, consider reflecting on them in the week that follows their respective presentation.

Reflect on the Apostles' Creed

Spend some time reflecting on the three articles of the Apostles' Creed. Consider how this creed is a remarkable summary of the Christian faith. If your tradition makes use of a catechism that relates to the Apostles' Creed, you might plan to read relevant passages from it. Also ask:

- How do we experience the triune God in creation?

- How do we experience Christ's gifts of redemption and reconciliation?

- How do we experience the Holy Spirit's renewal in our lives?

- How is professing our faith a way of life? What is enacted belief?

Reflect on the Lord's Prayer

Spend some time reflecting on the Lord's Prayer and of prayer in all its dimensions. Consider portions of a denominational catechism that relates to the Lord's Prayer or to prayer in general. Experience a wide range of prayer exercises. Explore possibilities for daily prayer, from simple prayers at waking and at bedtime to more formal practices of morning and evening prayer. Consider introducing a variety of prayer resources in weekly sessions (abbreviating and adapting them as necessary). Look at the prayers provided in the Small Group Blessings and Prayers section of this book (pages 149-155) and available as a separate handout on the companion CD-ROM. ⊙

Look Forward to Baptism or Affirmation of Baptism

Pay particular attention to the *renunciations* and to the *profession of faith*. Engage candidates in deep and personal considerations of what they are going to publicly renounce and affirm. Get specific. Ask:

- Where am I called to change? What in my life needs to die?

- What sinful desires draw me away from the love of God?

- What am I called to leave behind?

- Where do I need healing? How might my life be enlightened or illumined?

- What is the new life to which God is calling me?

- What does it mean for me to follow Jesus?

Expand the renunciations and profession of faith toward the communal or even cosmic dimensions of life and wonder together about the forces of wickedness and evil, and the church's call to bear witness together.

Consider the baptismal covenant or any vows or promises made in the baptism or affirmation of baptism service used by your congregation. See the baptismal covenant as a rule of life. Reflection on the baptismal covenant might continue in the weeks following baptism or affirmation of baptism. Begin to ask:

- How will I proclaim good news?

- How will I respect the dignity of every human being?

- What does it mean to strive for justice and peace?

- What impact does devoting myself to the community's worship have on me?

Retreat for Candidates and Sponsors

As candidates approach baptism or affirmation of baptism, one way to create additional time and space for reflection is to hold a retreat. The whirlwind surrounding a baptismal festival in congregational life can often be chaotic, but going on retreat for a little while in advance of baptism or affirmation of baptism can be a calm way to enter into a time that should be a highpoint in nearly everyone's life.

A retreat does not need to be a particularly lengthy time, perhaps five or six hours on the day before Passion (Palm) Sunday, or some Friday or Saturday evening through noon the next day (try not to miss worship with the rest of the congregation though). The point is to spend more time in spiritual reflection and in a less hurried atmosphere than may be possible during weekly sessions that are more dictated by the clock.

There is usually much to talk about nearer to baptism or affirmation of baptism. The additional suggestions in this book for sessions during the intense preparation stage will likely provide more than enough things to consider, making a retreat an ideal time to cover many of them.

A retreat need not be a costly endeavor. If you will not be going away overnight, perhaps simply going to another church just a few miles away in another community is enough to get out of the usual routine and spark some different questions or conversations as well. Nearby camping or retreat centers often provide accommodations at reasonable rates. If weather permits, an outing to a special outdoor setting may be desirable (perhaps even one near a significant body of water).

This might be a time to join up with another congregation or two that is also going through a similar process of making disciples. Perhaps a bishop or similar denominational leader will even be interested in joining you for a while, particularly if she or he is genuinely interested in listening to others in a faith formation process and entering into the spirit of the retreat.

Water Life: A Bible Study on Baptism and Water Images ●

This is a study that could be used as a way to prepare candidates for baptism or affirmation of baptism. It could also provide a way to reflect on baptism, particularly in the first week or two of Easter, especially if baptism was at the Vigil of Easter. Reflecting on all—or even most—of the scripture readings listed here would need to take place over several sessions.

Water is important for nourishing and sustaining life. In the Old and New Testaments we read about the life-giving properties of water and how it is also used in rituals of cleansing. Baptism—the Christian rite of initiation—brings together all these images. The apostle Paul wrote that we are cleansed of sin in baptism; but more than that, we die with Christ as our old sinful selves are drowned in the waters of baptism, while we rise with Christ to live in the promise of new life.

Reflection Questions

The scripture passages below are rich in images of water and baptism. As you read through them, reflect on the following questions:

- What is the significance of water in this passage?

- What point is the author trying to make?

- What might this passage say about the Christian life?

- What lessons are there to be learned?

- How is God speaking to me through this scripture passage?

- How can I apply this story to my own life and faith?

Biblical Passages

Genesis 1   *The creation story*

Genesis 7–9   *The flood story*

Exodus 14   *Moses and the crossing of the Red Sea*

Exodus 17:1-7; Numbers 20:1-13   *Water from the rock*

2 Kings 5:1-19   *Naaman cured in the Jordan River*

Isaiah 35:6; 41:17-20; 43:19-21; 58:11   *Water in the desert*

Matthew 3:13-17; Mark 1:9-11; Luke 3:21-22   *Jesus' baptism by John*

Matthew 8:23-25; Mark 4:35-41; Luke 8:22-25   *Jesus stills the storm*

Matthew 14:22-33; Mark 6:45-52   *Jesus walks on water*

Matthew 28:16-20   *Jesus gives the great commission*

John 2:1-11   *Jesus' first miracle—water changed into wine*

John 4:1-15   *Jesus and the woman at the well*

John 7:37-39; Revelation 22:1-21; Ezekiel 47:1-12   *River of living water*

Acts 2:1-42   *Mass baptisms on the day of Pentecost*

Acts 8:26-39   *Philip teaches and baptizes an Ethiopian*

Romans 6:1-11   *Baptism is dying and rising with Christ*

Preparation for Baptism and Affirmation of Baptism

- Work with anyone who may be responsible in planning rehearsals for worship leaders to include sponsors of any candidates for baptism or affirmation of baptism, whether it is for the Vigil of Easter or another occasion.

- Let the altar guild or sacristans know about additional arrangements that may be needed for baptism or affirmation of baptism, such as preparation of the font, use of oil and the paschal (Easter) candle, availability of baptismal candles, towels for the newly baptized, and places for those affirming their baptism to kneel.

- During one or more sessions with baptismal candidates just prior to baptism, speak with them about what they can anticipate in the baptism service, especially regarding the time of the service, its length (particularly if it is the Vigil of Easter), where they may gather and change their clothes (clothes for the baptism itself as well as dry clothes following), and if there will be a reception following the service to which they and their friends and families would be invited. Rehearse any specific responses that candidates for baptism may need to speak on their own (see Additional Suggestions for Sessions during the Stage of Intense Preparation, pages 116-118, regarding ways to reflect on the Apostles' Creed and the baptismal covenant or vows).

- If baptism will be by immersion or with significant amounts of water, candidates may wish to wear modest swimming attire and use a bathrobe for additional covering immediately before and after the baptism. A large bath towel should be available for each baptismal candidate to use in drying off following baptism. Consider where the newly baptized might go to change following baptism and what will transpire in the order of worship while the newly baptized are changing.

- Will candidates for affirmation of baptism be able to surround the baptismal font and use the water to remember baptism in any way (such as being invited to approach the font together with all the baptized in order to touch it and make the sign of the cross on themselves, or being sprinkled with water by the presiding minister and other worship leaders)?

- Consider the space where baptism will take place and be sure to have it well heated ahead of time (unless baptism is to occur in an outdoor location). If at all possible, try warming the water to a comfortable temperature for a swimming pool or a bath.

- Mark places in the worship folders for candidates and sponsors who need to be prepared to speak or to do certain actions, and review those items with participants just prior to the service.

- Instruct people who will be communing for the first time about the congregation's communion procedures.

- Prepare certificates of baptism and affirmation of baptism (confirmation) ahead of time for each candidate. Also prepare certificates or letters of thanks for sponsors as reminders of their responsibilities and commitments.

Baptismal Living

Snapshot of Baptismal Living ●

A time when the church rejoices with the newly baptized who now share with them the heart, mind, and work of Christ.

STAGE QUESTIONS: What does it mean to be a member of the body of Christ? How will you endeavor to follow Jesus Christ under the guidance of the Holy Spirit? What is your sense of calling to specific ministries? What support do you need in order to continue as Christ's faithful disciple?

ISSUES: Discovery of one's self as part of a sacramental community, discernment of spiritual gifts and specific sense of vocation(s), and clarity about ongoing participation in mutual support for the life of discipleship.

TIMELINE: This stage begins with focused attention for several weeks following baptism, though in reality it continues for a lifetime. If baptism occurs at the Vigil of Easter, this stage is observed during the fifty-day season of Easter, culminating with the Day of Pentecost.

PROCESS: Reflection on the sacraments just experienced and continuing discovery and discernment in worship, small group gatherings, prayer, service to others, and daily life ministry.

FOCUS: The church as a living embodiment of the risen Christ in worship, fellowship, and service.

CONGREGATION'S ROLE: Getting to know the newly baptized, affirming them in ministry, and inviting them into ongoing mutual accountability for discipleship.

Leads to ongoing participation in the life of the church using the disciplines that are basic to baptismal living: worship, prayer, scripture reflection, and service.

Reflection on Baptism or the Affirmation of Baptism

Very soon after baptism and affirmation of baptism (within a week is best), have a meeting so that the whole group can share their experiences with each other. Encourage people to speak about what touched them most deeply as well as what surprised them.

Help newly baptized and renewed Christians go deeper into their understanding of the sacraments and what participating in them means for daily living. If the primary sacramental elements have been used effectively, they should *speak* for themselves: water in a place of baptism that suggests a bath, bread and wine good enough for a feast. Help the newly baptized reflect upon their experiences of baptism and holy communion.

During gatherings with the newly baptized throughout the fifty days of Easter, consider the experience of the Vigil of Easter and its primary symbols, gestures, and actions. Recall the various movements (service of light, readings, baptism, communion) and the accompanying symbols. Ask:

- What did you experience?

- What did you see, touch, smell, taste, and hear?

- What did your experience teach you about God, Jesus, the Christian life or community?

- In light of your experience, how will you live differently?

Reflect on worship generally. Invite sustained reflection on participation in communion and all that takes place within the service.

- Study the communion liturgy, specifically the prayer of thanksgiving at the table, and discuss the implications that it has for daily living.

- Wonder together how sacramental living influences a person's relationships in all areas of life. How do we live gratefully and with a sense of Christian community and identity?

Baptismal Living Sessions

Continue in small or large group settings to dwell on the lectionary readings, using one or more methods of scripture reflection with which the group is already familiar, or explore additional possibilities in the Scripture Reflection Methods section (pages 140-143). Sacramental living is a prominent theme during the seven-week Easter season in all three years of the lectionary.

Explain to the newly baptized that they have now entered baptismal living, a stage that will continue for the rest of their lives. Explain the focus on discerning and using their gifts.

Ideas for the Easter Season

- During worship, the newly baptized could be set apart during the fifty days of Easter by wearing special symbols designed and given to them by the members of the congregation such as white robes or crosses.

- Include the newly baptized and those who have newly affirmed their baptism in the prayers of intercession (see examples on pages 174-175).

- Invite congregational members to reflect on Christian vocation in classes or on workshops that explore various aspects of ministry in daily life.

- Consider establishing groups for people in specific industries, fields of work, or areas of personal responsibility (education, health care, legal affairs, government, business, parenting, etc.) so that they might receive support from one another in the practice of their baptismal vocation. Such groups could meet in an ongoing basis on weekdays (maybe even for breakfast or on a lunch hour) and in locations that are close to people's workplaces.

- Include an affirmation of Christian vocation as a public rite for all the baptized, particularly on the Day of Pentecost. Such a rite may include an option for the newly baptized or newly affirmed to give testimony about their gifts and calling to ministry. Consider extending this opportunity to moments throughout the fifty days (or indeed at other times) for people to provide public testimony arising from their stories of conversion as well as to witness to the ways in which they see God using their gifts for ministry in the world. A few minutes of public witness after communion may provide a powerful context for the congregation to be blessed and sent forth into the world to love and serve God.

- Begin each Sunday of Easter with a thanksgiving for baptism or include a congregational renewal of baptismal vows. Sprinkle the assembly with water from the font or invite worshipers to the font to remember baptism in their own ways.

- Since numerous lectionary readings throughout the season of Easter in each of the three lectionary years relate to baptism or communion, preach on the sacraments frequently during this time. Relate the sacraments to baptismal living and life that is sustained by holy communion.

- Let the sacramental symbols of Easter be treated powerfully in the worship environment, prayers, and songs of the season.

- In addition to sessions with the newly baptized and those who have recently affirmed baptism, provide opportunities for others in the congregation to reflect upon the Vigil of Easter and how the movements, actions, gestures, signs, and symbols in it inform and shape Christian identity and living.

Mystagogical Reflection

What happens beyond baptism or affirmation of baptism? The goal of this stage is for the newly baptized and those who have recently affirmed their baptism to live in response to God's sacramental grace. The aim of this stage is to reflect on the mysteries of faith and the implications for daily living.

For Christian traditions practicing a form of making disciples called the *catechumenate*, the fourth and final stage is often known as *mystagogy* (**miss**-teh-goh-jee), a time for reflecting on deeper meanings of baptism and its significance for Christians' lives. *Mystagogical reflection* is guided and sustained contemplation of the church's worship, especially its sacraments, using biblical themes, images, and stories. Mystagogical reflection approaches baptism and communion as occasions when the triune God is the primary actor, bringing people to faith and new life. This type of reflection uses scripture to illuminate that mystery in such a way that it draws Christians to reflect on their experience in worship as an encounter with God, and then to consider the implications for behavior in daily life that reflects faith and belonging to Christ.

Mystagogical reflection follows participation in the rites and begins with recalling as fully as possible a specific experience of baptism, communion, anointing, or some other aspect of Christian worship. Using images from both scripture and daily life, the goal is to pile up meanings rather than to seek clear or rigid definitions. Images of baptism, for example, include tomb and womb, death and resurrection, absolution and new birth. Baptism heals, cleanses, washes, imparts the Spirit, incorporates into community, empowers for mission, and entrusts with vocation. Mystagogical reflection spells out implications for real life in the world. Living out our baptism compels us to:

* share life in community,
* practice hospitality,
* care for creation,
* provide for those in need,
* connect with Christians in unfamiliar settings, cultures, and circumstances, and
* relinquish certain attitudes and activities, including cultural notions of success, in the expectation that we will benefit by encountering Jesus Christ.

When baptism and affirmation of baptism occur at the Vigil of Easter, the period of baptismal living extends throughout the fifty-day Easter season and beyond. If the lectionary readings appointed for the Easter season are preached through the lens of the presence of the risen Christ in word and sacrament, the entire faith community can enter into worship as a time of mystagogical reflection that yields renewed baptismal living as God's Easter people.

The journey of faith continues beyond the moment of baptism as the congregation helps the newly baptized take the first steps on the path of discipleship by including them as full participants in the community, meditating on the gospel and sharing in communion together, and performing acts of charity and love. In these ways the congregation helps the newly baptized discern and use their gifts as part of the congregation's mission. This becomes a time when the newly baptized, together with the entire faith community, acquire more profound experiences of sharing in Christ's death and resurrection, both intellectually and in terms of lived, personal experience.

Ministry in Daily Life

The aim of the stage of baptismal living is discerning ministry in daily life. While the process leading up to baptism also considers the implications of Christian identity for all of life, this is a time to consider developing a few specific plans of action for living out baptism. Help the newly baptized and those who have recently affirmed their baptism to discover that we are nothing less than Christ's risen body given for the life of the world.

Help the newly baptized or renewed Christians discover their gifts for ministry, and help them pay attention to the various fields of mission in their daily lives: home, work, congregation, neighborhood, local community, and global community. A very helpful resource is *Living the Gospel: A Guide for Individuals and Small Groups* by A. Wayne Schwab and Elizabeth S. Hall (First Member Mission Press, 2010).

If your congregation culminates an intentional period of baptismal living with a rite of affirmation of vocation (perhaps on the Day of Pentecost), prepare participants for the rite. Have small group leaders, catechists, or sponsors prepared to speak about each person's gifts during this rite.

Exercises in Identifying Ministries in Daily Life

Use one or both of the following exercises in order to reflect on the ways in which members of the group minister in their daily lives.

Four Quadrants Exercise ●

- Take a single sheet of paper and mark it into four quadrants of equal size (a group leader can prepare sheets for all group members ahead of time). Label one of the quadrants *home*, a second quadrant *vocation*, a third quadrant *community*, and the fourth quadrant *world*.

- Have group members silently identify the roles that they play or actions that they perform in each of the four quadrants by writing words, drawing sketches, or making symbols in them (10 minutes).

- Ask group members to consider silently if there is balance between all four of the quadrants (3 minutes).

- Next ask group members to identify silently how God is involved in all four of the quadrants. How does God affect the choices and the priorities that they make in each quadrant (5 minutes)?

- Ask group members to consider silently what ways they might be more open to connections between their faith and daily life settings (5 minutes).

- Have group members draw their attention back to others in the group and ask each person to share briefly some of the words or pictures that he or she marked on the sheet (beginning with the group leader), as well as naming one thought about how he or she might achieve a better spiritual balance in life (15 minutes).

- Other questions that might be used to prompt discussion include:
    * Where is it easiest (or hardest) to incorporate God in your daily life? Why?
    * Who provides you with a good example of baptismal living? Why?
    * Share an example from your spiritual journey in which God opened up a new way to minister in daily life. What happened to make you ready?

- Allow participants to share as much or as little as they like. Passing is okay.

- Have participants spend a few moments on their own writing some goals for themselves on the reverse of the four quadrant sheet about the ways in which they believe that God is calling them to exercise their gifts for ministry in one or more of the quadrants (5-10 minutes).

- End the time together in group prayer.

The Trinitarian Shape of Ministry ❂

- Ask group members to imagine the various worlds or arenas that they each inhabit throughout the week: home, work, and community.

- Have group members silently consider which of their arenas is most actively present for them at 10:00 on a Tuesday morning. How is God's creative power (the first person of the Trinity) involved in their lives then (5 minutes)?

- Have group members take turns sharing aloud how they see God's creative power at work in their lives (5-10 minutes).

- Ask group members to imagine one of the other two arenas (home, work, or community) and a time of the week when they are most actively engaged in that arena. Have them silently consider how God's redemptive and restorative power (the second person of the Trinity) is at work in their lives then (5 minutes).

- Have group members take turns sharing aloud how they see God's redeeming and restorative power at work in their lives (5-10 minutes).

- Finally, ask group members to imagine the arena they have not yet considered (home, work, or community) and a time of the week when they are most actively engaged in that arena. How is God's enlivening and empowering Spirit (the third person of the Trinity) moving through them then (5 minutes)?

- Have group members take turns sharing aloud how they see God's enlivening and empowering spirit moving through their lives (5-10 minutes).

- Conclude with a prayer giving thanks for baptism and for the shape of God's trinitarian work in each person's life.

Preparation for the Rite of Affirmation of Vocation

- Determine who will speak about the gifts for ministry for each participant in the rite and rehearse it (speakers could include sponsors, catechists, small group leaders, or the team leader). The newly baptized may be included in the rehearsal.

- Provide the presiding minister with the rite and the musician with any music.

- Consider providing time in the rite for every member of the congregation to reflect upon their own gifts and how they are being used. This could be a time of silence, a time of testimony, or other invitation.

- Keep in mind that this is the final public rite of the disciple making process. A formal ending to the process and a clear commission to continued Christian living are helpful markers.

- Consider holding an adult forum or workshop in conjunction with this day to encourage everyone's active claim of their baptismal vocation in their various daily life settings.

Go Make Disciples

Beyond Baptism and Affirmation of Baptism

The point of making disciples is not simply to baptize new converts to the Christian faith or to guide people to affirm their baptism. People join the Christian community so that together they might all engage in God's mission to the world. A congregation that is not actively proclaiming God's love in word and deed will be challenged to do so by the presence of new Christians who take baptism seriously. Thus a ministry of making disciples does not just stop with welcoming new members; it is intended to revitalize the entire ministry of God's people for service in the world.

As a support to the newly baptized and to those who have re-entered the life of the church, congregations need to encourage such individuals in their faith development and service to the wider community. Each person should be connected to one or more particular ministries of the congregation within a few weeks following baptism or affirmation of baptism, if this has not already happened prior to that time. Congregations should provide focused follow-up with new disciples at several times within the first full year of membership. Sponsors may count on their commitments to last at least through the first year following baptism or affirmation of baptism. Having periodic reunions of small groups (three months, six months, twelve months, and each year thereafter) is a way of continuing to support them in their faith and lives of service.

Ultimately, all members of a congregation are regularly supported and encouraged in their call to be faithful in the covenant of baptism. Calls to see how people are doing could include the question, "How are you continuing in the faith of your baptism?"

Additional Resources

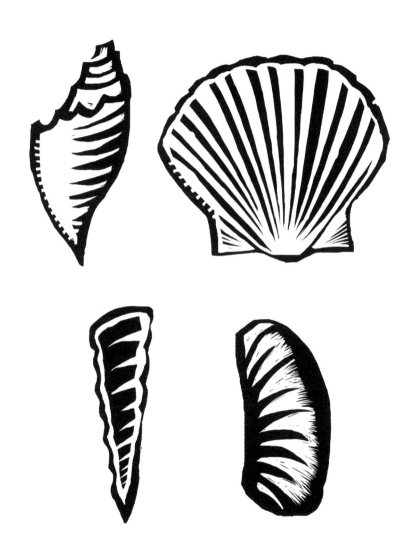

Scripture Reflection Methods

African Bible Study or *Collatio* ⬤

This method of scripture study is known in different circles by different names. The term *collatio* (coh-**lah**-tsee-oh) is derived from the Latin and refers to the process of "collecting" or gathering thoughts, reflections, and prayers through the hearing of a passage of scripture read multiple times. Another name for this method is African Bible Study, a reference to this practice among base Christian communities in South Africa. This method has been used with a great deal of satisfaction, especially when participants may have a limited reading ability. No matter what it is called, this method turns Bible study away from the intellectual pursuit of knowledge about the text and toward an attitude of listening to what God is saying through the text.

The outline of the process is adaptable at the discretion of the leader or the group, but it is important that the group share an understanding of the ground rules. In a society that takes little time to listen, it may take some practice for people to learn to listen carefully to the scriptures. Sharing of insights is encouraged. Debate or arguing points of interpretation is discouraged. Respecting the offerings of each individual is important. The group should agree to maintain trust and confidentiality with one another.

- The leader begins with an opening word that reminds the participants that Christ is present where we are gathered in his name. The leader then invites each person to listen carefully to the word as it speaks to them.

- The leader speaks a prayer of invocation.

- The selected passage is read slowly, distinctly, with pauses that allow hearers to dwell on the text.

- The group keeps silence for a few minutes of reflection.

- Participants are invited to share briefly a word, a phrase, or an image from the text that catches their attention and speaks to their life at this time.

- The passage is read a second time, slowly and deliberately.

- Silence is kept for a few minutes.

- Participants are invited to share about how the text speaks to a place in their lives that is deeper or wider. *Deeper* means reflecting more deliberately about some aspect of self that is challenged, questioned, or affirmed by the text. *Wider* means reflecting on how the text speaks about the person's relationships with others including family, work, and world.

- The passage is read a third time.

- Silence is kept for a few minutes.

- Participants are invited to speak a prayer that grows out of the text and their reflection on it. Sometimes the leader might encourage individuals to pray for themselves and other times they might pray for others in the group.

- The leader closes the session with prayer or a hymn.

Visualizing the Text ❂

In addition to hearing and reading a scripture passage, members of a group can visualize a text. Seeing a text acted out or drawn on a flip chart can take the passage out of the two-dimensional words and into a three-dimensional picture. A text portrayed visually or by persons acting it out takes on new life. Dialogue or ideas take shape, literally!

Relationships implied in the words of a text show up in visual relief. The group can even have fun by stretching a text into caricature in order to find the word that God addresses to them in the passage.

Almost any passage of scripture can be drawn or acted out. Parables of Jesus, stories from Acts, or accounts from the Old Testament provide a ready script. But the leader can help the group go beyond the initial impressions of the story by inviting them to stretch their perception of the passage. Notice the relationships and interplay of characters in the story. Then portray them using present-day language or with parallel images in today's society. Pay special attention to juxtaposition of characters. Draw the story in several frames in a cartoon format with thought balloons that express what is only implied in the words.

Other sections of scripture also lend themselves to visual expression. The psalms, the prophets, and many of the Pauline texts can be portrayed in drawing, acting, or sculpting as the storyline of the passage is identified one phrase, image, or sentence at a time.

The point of visualizing a passage is to help members of a group see the word of God as it is: lively, active, and speaking to their lives here and now. They might find themselves in a character of the story or in several characters. They might picture truths about their own lives that are illuminated by the acting out of the story. Because making disciples is about recognizing the call to faith and life in Christ, leaders can help groups find where the cross shows up in the story, either in fact or by asking what the story has to do with the death and resurrection of Jesus Christ.

Methods will vary according to the background, knowledge, and skills of the leader. Each group will develop its own sense of being together. Appropriate catechetical methods will help the group turn its attention to the word God is speaking to individuals and to the community of faith, to hear God's call to baptism and discipleship, and to respond affirmatively in faith.

Martin Luther's Four-Stranded Garland ◐

The following method, while initially presented by Martin Luther as an individual form of meditation in "A Simple Way to Pray," may also be adapted for use in groups in the following manner.

PREPARATION

- Select a passage from scripture.

- Allow group members to sit quietly and take a few minutes to relax.

- Let group members prepare themselves for prayer in ways they find most helpful.

- Encourage everyone to breathe deeply.

THE FIRST STRAND: INSTRUCTION

- Someone in the group reads the passage aloud slowly.

- Group members listen silently for the instruction they each hear from the text.
    * What is God saying to you?
    * Is there a word, a phrase, an image, or a feeling that captures you?

- Focus on the word, phrase, image, or feeling for a while before each person mentions it to the group in turn.

THE SECOND STRAND: THANKSGIVING

- Another person in the group reads the passage aloud slowly.

- Group members listen silently for something about which they would like to give God thanks.

- Group members allow feelings of thanksgiving to fill themselves.

- Group members each speak aloud about something for which they give thanks.

THE THIRD STRAND: WHOLENESS

- Another person in the group reads the passage aloud slowly.

- Group members listen silently for how the text is speaking to their dis-ease, woundedness, and sinfulness. Then group members speak aloud about how the text is speaking to their pain.

- Group members now listen silently for a word of comfort, healing, and forgiveness. Then group members speak aloud about how the text is speaking comfort, healing, and forgiveness to their pain.

THE FOURTH STRAND: PRESENCE

- Another person in the group reads the passage aloud slowly.

- Group members silently recall the word, phrase, image, or feeling from the first strand, resting in it and letting it lead them to rest in God.

CLOSING

Close with a group prayer of thanksgiving.

Supplemental Models for Disciple Making Sessions

Catechetical Sessions at St. Mark's Lutheran Church, San Francisco, California

DAY/TIME:	Sunday afternoon
DURATION:	75-90 minutes
STAGE:	Inquiry, Exploration, Intense Preparation, Baptismal Living

FORMAT:

15 min	Introductions, devotion/gathering activity
20-30 min	Dwelling in the Word focusing on the gospel reading from that morning
20-30 min	Formation using framing questions, handouts, and discussions
10 min	Prayer led by leader or participants as it develops

Notes: "Dwelling in the Word" is simply a form of scripture reflection. Questions of the participants are included in the formation period. Some of the framing questions include: Who is Jesus? How do we read the Bible? What is discipleship? St. Mark's has two cycles of formation sessions. The first concludes with baptisms and affirmations on All Saints Sunday, the second at the Vigil of Easter.

Catechetical Sessions at St. Michael and All Angels Episcopal Church, Portland, Oregon

DAY/TIME: Either Sunday afternoon or an evening early
                 in the week

DURATION: About 2 hours

STAGE: Exploration, Intense Preparation, Baptismal Living

FORMAT:

15 min	Taizé music for centering, brief worship, announcements
45 min	Small groups using scripture reflection on an upcoming gospel reading
10 min	Snacks
45 min	Bread for the Journey in large group; topic explored
5 min	Closing prayer

Notes: Opening worship quiets participants down. Brief worship includes scripture, spiritual writings, the prayer of the day, and intercessions. Small groups are made up of different people each week so that everyone gets to know everyone else. In Bread for the Journey, a topic is led by a team member and one of the resident clergy. There are no formal sessions in the Inquiry phase.

Catechetical Sessions at Bethlehem Lutheran Church, Auburn, California

DAY/TIME:	Wednesday evening
DURATION:	2 hours
STAGE:	Exploration, Intense Preparation, Baptismal Living

FORMAT:

30 min	Dinner
40 min	Small group scripture reflection focusing on an upcoming gospel reading
40 min	Large group discussion
10 min	Closing prayer

Notes: The sessions are in the context of a midweek congregational night with confirmation for teens and children's activities. All ages join in the meal. The inquiry phase does not include small groups and is open-ended. The format above applies to the remainder of the process. Large group topics are varied and sometimes relate to the lectionary readings. In Lent the focus is on the baptismal liturgy. During Easter the focus is on ministry in daily life. Closing prayer includes a variety of prayer forms.

Catechetical Sessions at Chelan Lutheran Church, Chelan, Washington

DAY/TIME:	Sunday after worship
DURATION:	45-60 minutes

STAGE: INQUIRY

FORMAT:

In the first session, take time to hear stories of arrival. How did you come to inquire about the Christian faith here and now? The rest of inquiry sessions go as follows:

10 min	Gathering activity. Physical movement is very helpful here.
20-30 min	*Here is what I don't get about God/Jesus/Church* . . . conversations centering on the questions and concerns of inquirers. Catechists must be ready with their own faith questions to encourage trust and depth. [Hint: These are conversations, not question-and-answer periods.]
15 min	Scripture reflection on the gospel text for the coming Sunday.
5 min	Assign homework and make it very simple. Notice how the theme of the day emerges in daily life this week.

TRANSITION TO EXPLORATION: RITE OF WELCOME

In the first meeting after each rite, check in with participants (15-20 minutes). How did you experience the rite?

STAGE: EXPLORATION

FORMAT:

15-20 min	Reports on homework. Expect great stories here!
15-20 min	Exploration of the liturgy. Teaching and conversation, one aspect of the liturgy per session (see below).
15 min	Scripture reflection on liturgy to bring the liturgy to the heart.
5 min	Assign homework.

CATECHESIS ON ONE ASPECT OF THE LITURGY

To invite people more deeply into worship and to explore how worship forms and equips for ministry, disciple making gatherings center on the exploration of the liturgy. Each week the focus is on one piece of the liturgy, following the order of the eucharistic rite, from the apostolic greeting to the Aaronic blessing. Each movement of the liturgy is examined, discussed, and prayed. Here the depth of the liturgy meets the richness of the catechetical process. Common life together, worshiping God, gathering around scripture, living into the tradition of the church, and partaking of the meal are all opened up to further exploration, prayer, and delight. Sponsors are reminded of the beauty and power of the liturgy and gain new appreciation for words and ritual that perhaps have become rote. Newcomers receive the gift of a rich welcome into the worship life of the congregation. In return they often offer wonderful insights into this new world they have entered.

TRANSITION TO INTENSE PREPARATION: RITE OF ENROLLMENT
See Rite of Welcome above.

STAGE: INTENSE PREPARATION
FORMAT:

15-20 min	Reports on homework.
15-20 min	Exploration of the liturgy.
15 min	Reflection on the liturgy.
5 min	Homework assignment.

Participation in mid-week Lenten services encouraged during this time.

TRANSITION TO BAPTISMAL LIVING: RITES OF BAPTISM AND AFFIRMATION
See Rite of Welcome above.

STAGE: BAPTISMAL LIVING
FORMAT:

15-20 min	Reports on homework.
15-20 min	Conversation on baptism, eucharist, and daily life.
10-15 min	Gifts within the body of Christ: types of spiritual gifts, discernment of gifts, and their use.
5 min	Homework assignment.

Affirmation of Vocation and the culmination of the disciple making process.

Notes: Sponsors often gain new or renewed appreciation for the beauty and power of the liturgy. During the scripture reflection portion of the session, ask each person to share a word or phrase that spoke to them. This is prayer with the liturgy.

Small Group Blessings and Prayers ◗

Prayers before Reading the Scriptures

Advent

Open your word to us, Lord God.
We wait for you and long to see your face,
for you are our rock, our safety, and our refuge.

Christmas

O Christ, enlighten my soul and heart with your never-setting light;
guide me to reverence of you, O Lord,
for your commandments are the light of my eyes.

Epiphany

Almighty God,
your Son has driven away darkness
with the brightness of your grace.
Enlighten all those who hear the word of life,
that they may be led by your truth
and walk in the brightness of the Morning Star,
Jesus Christ, in whose name we pray.

Lent

One thing I ask of the Lord;
one thing I seek;
that I may dwell in the house of the Lord all the days of my life.
–Psalm 27:4

Easter

I love you, O Lord my strength,
O Lord my stronghold, my crag, my haven;
my God, my rock in whom I put my trust.
My shield, the horn of my salvation and my refuge:
You are worthy of praise.
–Psalm 18:1-3

After Pentecost
Open our ears, that we may hear your word.
Open our eyes, that we may see your way.
Open our lips, that we may declare your praise.
Open our hearts, that your life may dwell among us.

November
As a deer longs for running streams,
so longs my soul for you, O God.
My soul is thirsting for you, O God,
when shall I come to appear before your presence?
–Psalm 42:1-2

Prayers and Thanksgivings after Reading and Praying the Scriptures

Advent
My soul proclaims the greatness of the Lord,
my spirit rejoices in God my Savior,
for you, Lord, have looked with favor on your lowly servant.
From this day all generations will call me blessed:
you, the Almighty, have done great things for me
and holy is your name.
You have mercy on those who fear you, from generation to generation.
You have shown strength with your arm and scattered the proud in their conceit,
casting down the mighty from their thrones and lifting up the lowly.
You have filled the hungry with good things and sent the rich away empty.
You have come to the aid of your servant Israel, to remember the promise of mercy,
the promise made to our forebears,
to Abraham and his children forever.
–Luke 1:46-55

Christmas

Now, Lord, you let your servant go in peace:
your word has been fulfilled.
My own eyes have seen the salvation
which you have prepared in the sight of every people:
a light to reveal you to the nations
and the glory of your people Israel.
–Luke 2:29-32

Epiphany

I put my trust in you, O God.
You grant your lovingkindness in the daytime;
in the night time your song is with me.
Send your light and your truth
that they may lead me.
Bring me to your holy hill
that I may go to your dwelling
and know the joys of your Son, Jesus Christ.

Lent

We thank you, holy Father, for your name
which you have made to dwell in our hearts,
and for the knowledge, faith, and immortality
which you have made known to us through your living Word, Jesus Christ.
To you be glory forever and ever.

Easter

Your words are as sweet as honey.
Your words are the delight of my heart. Alleluia!

After Pentecost

Your rain and snow come down from heaven, O God,
and they do not return until they have watered the earth,
making it sprout and grow.
Grant that your holy word take root in our lives
and accomplish in us your purposes,
through Jesus Christ our Lord.

November
As a swallow seeking a nest to hatch its young,
I am eager for your altar,
O Lord, my God.
In you, O God, my soul finds rest.
–Psalm 84:3-4

Prayers and Blessings to Conclude a Session
Advent
Devote yourselves to prayer,
and keep alert for the coming of the Lord.
The blessing of God, Father, Son, and Holy Spirit, keep you in peace.

Christmas
As God's chosen ones, holy and beloved,
clothe yourselves with compassion, kindness, humility, meekness, and patience.
Let the word of Christ dwell in you richly.
–Colossians 3:12, 16

Epiphany
Lord God of hosts,
we look for the day when you will set a feast for all your people,
a feast of rich food and well-aged wine,
a feast where no one will hunger or thirst,
a feast of grace and mercy in your Son, Jesus Christ.

Lent
O Lord, look with love on all who have been marked with the sign of the cross.
Lead them through the waters of baptism
and raise them up to new life with you,
that they may sing your praise
through your Son, Jesus Christ our Lord.

Easter
Lead a life worthy of your calling with all humility and gentleness,
with patience, bearing with one another in love,
making every effort to maintain the unity of the Spirit in the bond of peace.
–Ephesians 4:1-3

After Pentecost
May God strengthen you in the power of the Holy Spirit,
so that you may know the love of Christ, now and forever.

November
Rejoice always, pray without ceasing,
give thanks in all circumstances.
May the God of peace keep you sound and blameless
at the coming of our Lord Jesus Christ.
The one who calls you is faithful,
and he will do this.
–2 Thessalonians 5:16-17, 23-24

Additional Prayers and Blessings

Your face, O Lord, do I seek.
Do not hide your face from me.
–Psalm 27:8-9

Blessed Lord,
you speak to us through the holy scriptures.
Grant that we may hear, read, respect,
learn, and make them our own.
May your word grasp us, help us,
and hold us in hope.

Almighty God,
draw our hearts to you,
guide our minds,
fill our imaginations,
and control our wills
so that we may be wholly yours through Jesus Christ.

O Jesus,
be present with us
as you were present with your disciples.
Open to us the riches of your word
and enlighten us with your truth.

Good and gracious God,
send your word as good seed
into the fields of our hearts.
Let the gentle rain of your Spirit
bring to life the growth of faith within us.

The LORD bless you and keep you;
the LORD make his face to shine upon you, and be gracious to you;
the LORD lift up his countenance upon you, and give you peace.
–Numbers 6:24-26

May God be gracious to us and bless us and make his face to shine upon us.
–Psalm 67:1

May the God of peace make you complete in everything good
so that you may do his will,
working among you that which is pleasing in his sight, through Jesus Christ.
–Hebrews 13:20, 21

Be doers of the word, and not merely hearers.
–James 1:22

The grace of our Lord Jesus Christ be with you.
–1 Thessalonians 5:28

May the Lord of peace give you peace at all times in all ways.
–2 Thessalonians 3:16

The grace of the Lord Jesus Christ,
the love of God,
and the communion of the Holy Spirit be with all of you.
–2 Corinthians 13:13

The peace of God, which surpasses all understanding,
keep your hearts and your minds in Christ Jesus.
–Philippians 3:7

May your love overflow more and more with knowledge and full insight
to help you determine what is best,
so that in the day of Christ
you may be pure and blameless,
having produced a harvest of righteousness that comes through Jesus Christ
for the glory and praise of God.
–Philippians 1:9-11

We give thanks to God for you,
brothers and sisters, as is right,
because your faith is growing abundantly,
and the love of every one of you is increasing.
–2 Thessalonians 1:3

Beloved,
build yourselves up on your most holy faith;
pray in the Holy Spirit;
keep yourselves in the love of God;
look forward to the mercy of our Lord Jesus Christ.
–Jude 20-21

Peace be with you.
–John 20:21

Rehearsing the Rites

No matter what liturgical celebrations we are preparing there are always a few basic rules of performance that require some attention. Though the liturgy is not exactly comparable to a theatrical performance, nevertheless, for a rite to strike the heart attention needs to be given to its enactment. In liturgical traditions that flow out of the Reformation period, the spoken word has often been privileged over the ritual word. This piece addresses ritual: the enacted, visible, and tangible word.

All of the rites used in making disciples involve welcome or welcoming back to a community of faith. In other words, all of the rites involve people versed deeply in the community and also those not as familiar with it, perhaps even nervous about public manifestation of the faith. Rehearsal in these circumstances is paramount. It offers a chance for even the seasoned worship leader to see where something might go awry.

How much rehearsal is necessary for the candidates? Of course explaining the basic order and also what is expected of the candidates is certainly desirable (where will they stand, what responses will be expected, etc.), yet the extent of this preparation or rehearsal requires considerable thought. Part of the power of any ritual is its unexpected quality. Good ritual enables a participant to step into a process of discovery while it is happening. A balance needs to be found for providing inquirers or candidates with enough information that will ensure their comfortable participation, yet still enable them to experience the rites firsthand without a lot of foreknowledge. After each rite there should be opportunity for a rehearsal after the fact as the ritual is debriefed and the candidates enter into preparation for the next stage. In the early church this process of rehearsing afterward was called *mystagogical catechesis*. Today we understand or speak about it as baptismal living. The practice of not fully rehearsing with the candidates ahead of time is an invitation to trust.

A pastor recounts this story. One woman who was to be baptized called at the beginning of Holy Week to say that she wanted to change some of the baptismal liturgy and needed to know what exactly was going to happen. The pastor responded by inviting her to trust that the Spirit was working and that she might want to let go of control. In that moment it all clicked for her. Many years later, this is the story she tells as a key turning point in her faith. There was a profound surrender in her that continues to echo in her life of faith.

What Elements of Rehearsal Need to Be Considered?

MATERIALS

There is nothing as embarrassing as handing out Bibles or catechisms and not having enough! What things do you need for the rites that are being engaged? This includes everything from the most evident (for example, having enough water in the font—something that should be checked regularly whether or not there is a baptism) to oil for anointing or clean albs for the newly baptized. In the case of oil for anointing (usually olive oil) you may also wish to scent it with bergamot or some other natural scent that leaves a lasting, fragrant reminder of the Spirit flowing in and through our existence. Make a list of things that you need and check it off.

SPACE

How are you going to use the space (sanctuary, narthex, hall, outside area)? How are you going to navigate it? Choreography is important and needs to be practiced. Begin by figuring out who is most directly involved. How many participants are there? Is there enough space? Where will they stand and in what formation? Do the presiding and assisting ministers have enough space to move around? Perhaps the space needs to be rearranged (moving chairs, etc.). If outside, can the participants be heard? In what direction are people facing?

GESTURES AND SPEECH

Once again, you will want to think about what gestures, movements, and speech need to be rehearsed. Practicing responses with candidates never hurts. Who is doing what? Who is saying what? Is an acolyte or assisting minister required for holding the presiding minister's worship book? If so, figure out on what side she or he should stand and even at what level someone else should hold the book.

WHO

It is important to think about who else might be included in the ritual but not necessarily directly involved. Are there children, parents, or significant others? Are they to be invited to the font or the altar or wherever the ritual action is taking place?

FLOW

Rites used to mark the process of making disciples are usually part of a regular worship service, primarily on a Sunday. Their placement is established by various denominational worship resources, but this does not ensure an easy flow, especially if the rites are only enacted occasionally. It is important to think through the connections between weekly ritual actions and the occasional rites. Who leads the transition? Is there a dead time? How will you deal with it? Sometimes silence is welcome, but not if leaders are fumbling with something or otherwise uncomfortable with it. If you are a presiding minister, a liturgist, or another person responsible for leading worship, you may wish to sit quietly at some point before a worship service and walk through it in your mind, double checking how connections are being made between various parts. How does the flow feel?

MUSIC

Considering the flow of the service will usually mean consulting with a church musician. What does she or he need to know? It may be advisable to have a director of music at the rehearsal. The church musician can help in transitioning both into and out of the rites.

CONGREGATION

While a congregation may not actually rehearse a rite it can still be prepared ahead of time. Rites of welcome, enrollment, baptism, and others can be announced ahead of time, with explanations given about their significance. A sermon can serve as instruction about what the congregation is preparing to do or has just done. Reflecting on the lectionary readings for any given Sunday can also help to connect the rites with God's unfolding story in a congregation's life. How can the readings, sermon, and announcement times introduce the congregation to the meaning and practice of the rites of making disciples?

PRESIDING MINISTER

The presiding minister continually rehearses the role of John the baptizer. That is, the presiding minister continually points toward Christ and the central things in the gathered assembly, but away from herself or himself. The presiding minister is not a mediator between God and the people. Nor is the presiding minister in the role of a popular television host or entertainer (though many people come to church expecting and subsequently judging the presiding minister on his or her entertainment skills). The presiding minister is none of these: not mediator, not ancient/sacred priest, not entertainer, not dispenser of heavenly wisdom. The presiding minister is witness—witness to a baptismal reality already present in the assembly. The presiding minister empowers the assembly to claim its calling as the body of Christ that welcomes new disciples into its midst. The presiding minister as witness is called upon to expand and deepen the participation of the assembly in the work of proclaiming the gospel and witnessing to Jesus Christ. Catechesis is intimately linked to the liturgical celebration. Finally, the presiding minister also rehearses through private meditation and prayer.

A Word to Preachers

If welcoming new disciples is to be anything more than a side dish in the fare of church life, preaching must spark a vision that invigorates the great commission itself in the life of a congregation. A fruitful process of making disciples requires a faith community willing and able to accompany and incorporate people into the life of Christ. So how can the preacher help shape such actions?

PLACE PRIMARY FOCUS ON THE GOD TO WHOM THE BAPTIZED AND BAPTISMAL CANDIDATES ALIKE HAVE BEEN ATTRACTED

What God has done in the life, death, and resurrection of Christ is foundational to all that we are and do as Christians. This God is active in the lives and contexts of those who listen to our sermons too, therefore preaching must speak explicitly of God's gracious presence and activity in the scriptures and in the world today. People adept at guiding others into the way of Christ are increasingly able to articulate how God is at work in their own lives and recognize how God may be active in the lives of inquirers.

As you prepare your sermon in light of a biblical text or liturgical action, ask:

* Where is God in or behind this text or action? What is God/Christ/the Holy Spirit up to here?
* What characteristic of Christ or aspect of God's nature does this text or action reveal or suggest?
* What or whom does God care about?
* What is God promising for the world?
* Where are these attributes of God evident in the context and experience of the world, the church, or inquirers today?

INTERPRET THE COMMUNITY OF FAITH TO WHICH INQUIRERS HAVE BEEN ATTRACTED

In this day and age, those drawn to the way of Christ are not usually attracted to a system of beliefs or a philosophical construct of ideas, but rather to a particular community of people whose welcome or way of life they have found compelling. Therefore, preaching must demonstrate how the narrative of God's loving action continues to be written in and through the community of faith. The ancient catechumenate emerged in a church that believed a new creation had begun in the resurrection of Jesus. That church understood itself as participating in God's promised and emerging reign of reconciliation, justice, and peace. The catechumenate became the process by which those coming to faith were resocialized to live by this new order. A community proficient at guiding others into the way of Christ is one that increasingly comprehends and orients its practices in light of this understanding. Preaching should become a lens through which a congregation can survey its practices from such a perspective. In sermon preparation ask yourself:

* In what particular activity of the church do we continue or reflect a practice seen or exhorted in the scripture text?
* How does a particular activity of our congregation anticipate or participate in the promised and imminent reign of God? How does it reflect what God cares about?
* How does a particular rite of discipleship invite or shape inquirers and congregation alike for the reign of God?
* How does a text or liturgical action challenge our current understandings or practices?
* Does the sermon present the baptismal life as one that reflects and witnesses to God's promised reign?

MIRROR THE PROCESS OF FORMATION AND DISCOVERY EMBODIED BY THE PROCESS OF MAKING DISCIPLES ITSELF

The homily should attend regularly to the religious experience of inquirers, echoing something of the process of discovery in which they are engaged. Likewise, the journey and experience of new disciples can be held before the congregation just as the congregation's example is commended to them. As the eucharistic table aspires to be the ritual embodiment of what we are called to be and do at the tables of our lives, the sermon can serve as a ritual embodiment of the process of making disciples, of being shaped by the word in and for daily living.

In shaping a sermon consider:

* Does the sermon pay attention to the questions and struggles, insights and experience of inquirers and others in the congregation who have engaged this text in the past week, or who will engage it in the week ahead?
* Does the sermon's plot complement the process followed in your congregation's catechetical sessions?
* If a particular rite of the process of making disciples is to be celebrated, does the sermon prepare worshipers for it without becoming didactic or explanatory? If a rite has been celebrated already, does the sermon prompt its memory, evoke its symbols and actions, or foster listeners' reflection on their experience of it?

* What do you hope your listeners will experience? What is it that you expect God will do as a result of your sermon? State this for yourself in one clear sentence.

INVITE LISTENERS TO TAKE AN ACTIVE ROLE IN THE MINISTRY OF MAKING DISCIPLES

Sermons are seldom effective in inspiring Christian belonging and practice if they simply offer ruminations about how this Sunday's readings might be applied in the week ahead. It usually proves ineffective, too, if sermons place primary focus on what we are called to be or do. Therefore, the invitation to engage in the work of making disciples will most likely be embraced if issued as a response to what God has done, is doing, and will do for the life of creation and in the lives of those called to faith. Nevertheless, the invitation must be made. Likewise, practical suggestions need to be offered for making disciples and not just adding members.

As you consider your preaching ministry overall, ask yourself if you address the following questions for the life of the congregation on a regular basis:

* What does it look like to welcome with biblical hospitality those who enter our midst as strangers or inquirers?

* How can or do we model the Christian life for those who are responding to the gospel's invitation?

* How might we walk with or tutor those who look to us for deepening understandings of a God whom they have recognized as active in their lives, the God to whose loving action they yearn to respond?

FINALLY, ASK YOURSELF

Am I as a preacher explicitly inviting listeners to become involved in the welcome and formation of inquirers, candidates for baptism, the newly baptized, or those renewing their baptismal faith?

Preaching to Catechumens

Preaching to catechumens was an important tool for forming Christians in the early church. In many instances these sermons were preached following baptism. The newly baptized would gather in the week after Easter to debrief their experience. The preacher would honor their experience by helping them recall the sights, sounds, symbols, actions, and gestures surrounding their baptism. Vivid examples of such sermons by John Chrysostom, Ambrose of Milan, Theodore of Mopsuestia, and Cyril of Jerusalem are found in resources such as *The Awe-Inspiring Rites of Initiation: Baptismal Homilies of the Fourth Century,* edited by Edward Yarnold, s.j.

These preachers would ask: What did you see? What did you hear? What did you do? Drawing upon the experience of the newly baptized, they would help new Christians reflect upon their experience of the sacraments in order to draw out their deeper meaning. Instead of explaining baptism or holy communion before participating in them, these ancient preachers allowed the newly baptized to experience them first. For example, Ambrose honored this approach so that "the light of the sacraments be inculcated in the candidates as surprise" (Craig A. Satterlee in *Ambrose of Milan's Method of Mystagogical Preaching*). Known as *mystagogy* or study of the mysteries, this style of preaching and teaching helps the newly baptized reflect on the rites in which they have participated. This is borne of the conviction that worship itself teaches us. The emotional and spiritual impact of the rites leading to baptism, the bath itself, or participating in holy communion evokes a sense of wonder and awe which is life-giving. Instead of offering explanations, we invite catechumens and the newly baptized to reflect upon their experience. William Harmless concurs:

> Explaining rites can easily lapse into explaining them away…. Mystagogical catechesis is thus less an explanation and more an exploration; it is less an explication and more an evocation. It works like sonar: it plumbs the depths not to deny the depths, but rather to point out how deep they actually are. (William Harmless, s.j., *Augustine and the Catechumenate*)

In helping participants explore the rites, preachers would connect them to stories and images from the Bible, the prevailing culture, and the natural world. In this way preachers would proclaim what God was actively doing in the rites themselves and in the lives of the catechumens and the newly baptized. The good news of God's saving activity was proclaimed. God, whose work of salvation took place through

Israel and in Jesus Christ, continues this saving work at the font and in and among the community gathered around the table.

How might these ancient practices apply today? Since making disciples is marked by a series of public rituals, it is wise to take the time to explore the rites with the participants. For example, following the rite of welcome, the leader will help participants during the next catechetical session to recall all that occurred: the signing of the cross on the body, the presentation of a Bible, the welcoming by the community, the blessing prayer. Invite catechumens, affirmers, and sponsors to name their experience; what they did, saw, and heard. Ask them what they were feeling or thinking when the cross was traced on their bodies or they received the Bible and the invitation to honor its mysteries. Identify how God was at work in these liturgical rites. Once this has taken place, the pastor or catechist may preach a short sermon to catechumens, affirmers, and sponsors. He or she would incorporate the insights shared from the group and then redescribe the experience of the rite and so proclaim the good news. The preacher could describe the actions of the rite by tapping into a wide array of stories and images. For example, the preacher would relate the signing of the cross to the various ways we mark our bodies with tattoos, make-up, lipstick, or cologne; or how we receive purposeful touch from a kiss, handshake, or embrace. Then the preacher could relate the signing of the cross to Jesus' call to take up our cross and follow him and note how this same sign of the cross is made over the entire assembly each Sunday, as well as proclaim the various ways we receive God's holy touch through such things as anointing, the sharing of the peace, or receiving bread and cup.

If baptism occurs at the Vigil of Easter, each catechetical session following with the newly baptized could conclude with worship in which the various movements and actions of the Vigil are recalled. This could include a short sermon on one or more of the symbols: the lighting of the paschal (Easter) candle, the Easter proclamation, service of readings, bath, anointing, thanksgiving prayer, communion, and so on.

In addition to catechetical sessions with the newly baptized, preaching to inquirers, catechumens, and affirmers might take place within the worship of the gathered assembly. It would do no harm—in fact, it would be tremendously helpful—for the supporting congregation to hear. Perhaps a sermon on one of the rites would be appropriate in the context of the Sunday celebration in which it is taking place. For example, when those preparing for baptism sign their names in a book on the day when the rite of enrollment is held, the preacher could cite examples of how we sign our names to important documents to declare our endorsement or commitment and then draw upon the imagery of Revelation and proclaim that these baptismal candidates' names were being written in God's book of life. When the supporting congregation overhears such a word, they are inspired to greater support of candidates and reflect upon their own lives of faith. In a style consistent with ancient practice, a rite may precede the sermon that would serve to reflect on the experience.

The lectionary readings during the season of Easter, filled with sacramental images, implore us to reflect upon the gift of the sacraments. The preacher, on any given Sunday during this fifty-day season, could address the newly baptized or those who have renewed their baptismal vows, and the rest of the assembly could not help but make the connections to their own experiences through liturgy and daily life.

Sampling the Ecumenical Rites

Ecumenical Resources and Rites

Since the initial recovery of the catechumenate in the 1980s (see Cata-What? A Brief History of the Catechumenate, pages 183-185) a number of denominations have adopted the approach of making disciples explored in this handbook. The section that follows provides a list of the rites of initiation from several churches in Canada and the United States. Each church has cast its resources in ways that reflect that tradition's approaches to liturgy and formation. The resources are like branches on a single trunk providing each denomination with a way to baptism and affirmation of baptism: Christ forming his body journey by journey, baptism by baptism, congregation by congregation.

Why should I care about ritual resources other than those my own denomination offers? Of course your denomination's rites are primary. The resources of other churches may be very similar, almost identical. Others may be quite different. Either way, looking at how other churches approach ritualizing the journey next to your own church's way to baptism may enable you to find an "aha!" that deepens your understanding. It may even spark a more richly nuanced way of enacting a rite in your context. The invitation here is to know your own denomination's rites well and to widen your awareness and appreciation of the wider horizon of how others enact journeys of discipleship.

What the Resources Have in Common

- **A series of stages and ritual moments.** Each church's rites are the ritual moments that conclude one stage of formation and lead into the succeeding period, the last being baptismal living that continues for a lifetime.

- **The basic outline is the same.** As we have already seen, the journey to discipleship begins with searches prompted by the Spirit's wooing and working in people's lives. When seekers' journeys ripen toward and in a church, congregations welcome the seekers and ask them to commit to a time as apprentices, sharing the worship, scripture reflection, prayer, and ministry of the congregation in the world. When apprentice relationships reach the point of readiness to commit to a way of life and baptism, catechumens are enrolled for baptism. With the date of baptism announced to people who have and will continue to pray for them, baptismal candidates enter the most intense portion of the journey into Christ. At the Vigil of Easter, or other day of baptism, candidates are initiated into Christ's royal priesthood in the rites of baptism, laying on of hands/anointing, and eucharist. Now apprentices begin the lifelong mastery of self in service to Christ in the world. The sacraments shape the journey in the days and weeks immediately following the experience of initiation. The newly baptized explore the baptismal covenant and make deepening connections with their new life in Christ. Some churches invite the newly baptized to celebrate and affirm their vocation of ministry in the world a few weeks following baptism.

What Is Different from Rite to Rite?

- **Terminology:** each church's rites have different names for the rites of initiation.

- **Number of rites:** For adults preparing for baptism (the catechumenate) some churches have three primary ritual moments and some have four. For example, the Anglican and Episcopal churches have welcome, enrollment, and baptism. The Evangelical Lutheran Church and United Methodists add a fourth rite: affirmation of vocation.

- **Amount of commentary:** As you explore the resources, you will note that some offer very simple ritual texts without much commentary on what precedes and follows the liturgical action. Others offer a good deal of commentary and direction on both the rites and the stages or periods of formation that precede and follow each rite. The Mennonite Church and Reformed Church in America offer brief commentary. Roman Catholics and United Methodists provide more commentary.

- **Additional rites in stage three:** Some churches provide specific additional prayers and acts during the third stage of handing on the faith and prayer of the church, while others do not.

- **Alternative tracks:** Some resources provide a primary *track* for adult candidates for baptism, with additional tracks provided for various other people with different needs :

    baptized persons seeking to affirm/reaffirm the baptismal covenant (for example Anglican, Episcopal, Evangelical Lutheran, Roman Catholic, United Methodist)

parents desiring to bring their children for baptism (for example Anglican, Episcopal, United Methodist).

Making Best Use of Your Tradition's Rites

- **Adapt to your setting:** denominational liturgies have to be suited to the local setting. Your worship space, the age, gender, and abilities of your inquirers, the degree of formality, how scripted or unscripted worship in your setting is, and how graceful and comfortable your people are with ritual action will require adaptation of the printed rites. Whether or not your denomination requires or recommends use of the rites will influence how free you are to adapt them.

- **Stay the course:** Don't be afraid to lean into the rites and use them with the best flair and love you can muster. Remember, external actions shape internal emotions and responses. A little water has little effect. A lot of water changes lives and will never be forgotten! Fragrant oil lavishly smeared over hair and face communicates powerfully. All of the rites call for actions that you enact graciously and powerfully.

- **Keep the big picture in mind:** Forming disciples is a relational journey, not another church program. In every person God is longing for life and love, belonging, and purpose. Attending to God's longing in others is prelude and foundation to evangelization and the process of making disciples. The greatest temptation for most of us will be to get excited about how cool this might be and to treat it as another layer of church activity, when baptizing men and women into the reign of God begs to be a central feature of congregational life. It is not about church growth; it is about welcoming seekers and forming disciples. A faithful ministry of making disciples welcomes God adding living stones into the spiritual house (1 Peter 2:5).

Denominational Rites for Making Disciples

This is a list of major denominational traditions in North America that have produced rites for making disciples or for the adult catechumenate. Several other traditions have also produced rites for baptism, confirmation, and affirmation or reaffirmation of baptism. Rites listed here have varying levels of status or authority within their respective traditions; some are approved, while others are authorized, canonical, or commended, and still others are provisional. A church's primary approved, authorized, canonical, or commended rites are listed first, while other provisional rites follow. When a church has developed approved, authorized, canonical, or commended rites, then any similar provisional rites that had been produced previously are not mentioned. When a church has supplemented its approved, authorized, canonical, or commended rites with other provisional rites, both are indicated.

Anglican Church of Canada

The Book of Alternative Services (1985)
- Holy Baptism
  * The Baptismal Covenant
  * At Confirmation, Reception, or Reaffirmation
- Confirmation

Making Disciples: The Catechumenate in the Anglican Church (1991/2011)
- Rites of Initiation
  * Welcoming Inquirers or Families as Apprentices
  * Calling Apprentices to Be Baptismal Candidates
  * Holy Baptism [elements that enrich the *BAS* rite]
- Rites of Turning Again to Christ
  * Welcoming Those Who Are Again Turning to Christ
  * Ash Wednesday: A Call to the Life of Conversion
  * Maundy Thursday: Restoring Communion in Mutual Service
  * Reaffirmation of the Baptismal Covenant [enriching the *BAS* rite]

The Episcopal Church

Book of Common Prayer (1979)
- Holy Baptism
  * The Baptismal Covenant
  * Confirmation, Reception, or Reaffirmation
- Confirmation with forms for Reception and for the Reaffirmation of Baptismal Vows

The Book of Occasional Services (2003)
- Preparation of Adults for Holy Baptism: The Catechumenate
  * Admission of Catechumens
  * During the Catechumenate
  * Enrollment of Candidates for Baptism
  * During Candidacy
  * The Presentation of the Creed
  * The Presentation of the Lord's Prayer
- A Vigil on the Eve of Baptism
- Preparation of Baptized Persons for Reaffirmation of the Baptismal Covenant
  * Welcoming Returning Members and Members Baptized in Other Traditions
  * Enrollment for Lenten Preparation
  * Maundy Thursday Rite of Preparation for the Paschal Holy Days
- The Preparation of Parents and Godparents for the Baptism of Infants and Young Children

Evangelical Lutheran Church in America (ELCA)
Evangelical Lutheran Church in Canada (ELCIC)
Evangelical Lutheran Worship (2006)
- Holy Baptism
- Welcome to Baptism
- Affirmation of Baptism
- Affirmation of Christian Vocation

Renewing Worship (vol. 3): *Holy Baptism and Related Rite*s (2002)
- Formation in Faith Related to Baptism
  * Enrollment of Candidates for Baptism
  * Blessing of Candidates: Confession of Faith
  * Blessing of Candidates: Renunciation of Evil
  * Blessing of Candidates: Commitment to Prayer
  * Affirmation of Christian Vocation
- Formation in Faith Related to Affirmation of Baptism
  * Welcome of Inquirers
  * Call to Renewal
  * Preparation for the Three Days
  * Affirmation of Christian Vocation

Mennonite Church USA
Welcoming of New Christians: A Guide for the Christian Initiation of Adults
(1995)
- Service of Welcome
- Service of Decision
- Service of Baptism

Presbyterian Church (U.S.A.)
Cumberland Presbyterian Church
Book of Common Worship (1993)
- The Sacrament of Baptism
- An Alternative Service for the Sacrament of Baptism
- Baptism and Reaffirmation of the Baptismal Covenant: A Combined Order
- Reaffirmation of the Baptismal Covenant for Those Making a Public Profession of Faith
- Reaffirmation of the Baptismal Covenant for Those Uniting with a Congregation
- Reaffirmation of the Baptismal Covenant for a Congregation
- Reaffirmation of the Baptismal Covenant Marking Occasions of Growth in Faith
- Reaffirmation of the Baptismal Covenant in Pastoral Counseling

Reformed Church in America
Companions on the Way (2005)
- Journey Celebrations
  * [Welcome] Bible Presentation and Signing with the Cross
  * [Adult Baptism] Order for the Profession of Faith
  * [Sending] A Service of Affirmation of Ministry in Daily Life

Roman Catholic Church
Rite of Christian Initiation of Adults (1972, 1985)
- Christian Initiation of Adults
  * Acceptance into the Order of Catechumens
  * Election or Enrollment of Names

- * Rites Belonging to the Period of Purification and Enlightenment
  - Scrutinies
  - Presentation of Creed
  - Presentation of the Lord's Prayer
  - Preparation Rites on Holy Saturday
- * Celebration of the Sacraments of Initiation
  - Celebration of Baptism
  - Celebration of Confirmation
  - Renewal of Baptismal Promises
- Rites for Particular Circumstances
  - * Christian Initiation of Children Who Have Reached Catechetical Age
  - * Christian Initiation of Adults in Exceptional Circumstances
  - * Christian Initiation of a Person in Danger of Death
  - * Preparation of Uncatechized Adults for Confirmation and Eucharist
  - * Reception of Baptized Christians into Full Communion of the Catholic Church

Rite of Baptism for Children (1969)
Rite of Confirmation (1971)

The United Methodist Church

The United Methodist Book of Worship (1992)
- Services of the Baptismal Covenant
  - * Holy Baptism
  - * Confirmation
  - * Reaffirmation of Faith
  - * Reception of Members
  - * Congregational Reaffirmation

Come to the Waters (1996)
- Initiation of Adults
  - * Welcoming Hearers
  - * Calling Persons to Baptism
  - * Prayers and Rites during the Final Preparation
  - * Handing on the Faith of the Church

- * Handing on the Prayer of the Church
- * Examination of Conscience
- * Affirmation of Ministry in Daily Life
- Initiation of Children
  - * Welcoming a Child as a Hearer
  - * Calling Children to Baptism through the Parent(s)
  - * Confirmation and Affirmation of Ministry in Daily Life
- Persons Returning to the Baptismal Covenant
  - * Welcoming a Returning Member
  - * Calling the Baptized to Continuing Conversion
  - * Reconciliation on Holy Thursday
  - * Affirmation of Ministry in Daily Life

Constructing a Temporary Font

Although a font large enough for baptism by immersion will ordinarily be a permanent installation in a congregation's worship facilities, congregations that have not been able to renovate their space or that are in the process of acquiring their own worship space may wish to consider how an adequate baptismal space can be improvised.

Some congregations have provided temporary baptismal spaces either to accommodate the baptism of adults upon occasion or to celebrate major baptismal festivals throughout the year, particularly at the Vigil of Easter. On those occasions when the assembly may experience a stational liturgy (such as the Vigil of Easter, when the assembly may be moving from a place outdoors for the lighting of the new fire to other spaces in the church building for the service of readings, baptism, and the celebration of the meal), it is not even necessary that a baptismal space be within the room in which the assembly normally worships.

A fellowship hall or gathering space may provide a suitable location for a temporary font. Set a portable wading pool (as plain as possible), a large galvanized tub, or a sturdy water tank on the floor, with plenty of space for an assembled congregation to gather around. Though the container may not be able to accommodate the full immersion of an adult, it may be possible for baptismal candidates to kneel in the water while the presiding minister pours water from a pitcher or a baptismal ewer over their heads. Candidates for baptism may be dressed in swimwear for the baptism itself and may also have a bathrobe that they use prior to and immediately following the baptism (allow them time to change from and into an alb or street attire for other portions of the service).

Make the space surrounding a temporary font visually appealing. Gather large green plants (but not much taller than whatever is used to hold the water) around the temporary font, while still making it easy for candidates and ministers to approach the font. Ideally the water in the font would be slightly warmer than room temperature. Partially fill the tub with water hours (or even a day) in advance of when it is to be used. Then add warmer water to the font within an hour ahead of time so that it is up to a comfortable temperature, similar to a bath or a swimming pool.

Any size font and any amount of water may technically do the job for the celebration of baptism, however the fullest use of water that is possible will convey an image of God's abundant grace in this sacrament in an expansive and vivid way, exemplifying the words and actions of the baptismal service.

Praying for Those Preparing for Baptism and the Newly Baptized ❂

Pastors and other congregational leaders may want to surround those baptized in their assemblies with prayer. The weekly prayers of intercession offer a wonderful opportunity to lift before God candidates who are preparing for baptism, as well as those who have been recently baptized. Congregations do well to pray for candidates, their sponsors (godparents), and their families *before* and *after* baptism. After all, the assembly makes that promise—to support and pray for the newly baptized—in the rite of baptism itself.

Prayers of intercession are best prepared locally for each occasion; however, the following model intercessions may be used throughout the year, and adapted or edited to fit the particular needs of your congregation. A petition for the newly baptized fits well early on, following prayers for the church universal, or later on, during congregational petitions. Pastors who are aware of upcoming baptisms should remember to share this information with assisting ministers or other laypersons who help prepare the Sunday intercessions for the assembly.

Sample Petitions

Praying during Lent for those who will be baptized at the Vigil of Easter:
During this season of Lent, we pray for people everywhere who will be born again in the waters of baptism at the Vigil of Easter. Especially, we pray for *name/s*. Surround *them, their families,* and *their sponsors/godparents* with a love that knows no bounds.

Praying, during preceding weeks, for those who will be baptized on one of the other baptismal festivals of the church year or on another Sunday:

> *Baptism of Our Lord*
> O God, you poured out your Spirit on your Son in the waters of the Jordan.

> *Pentecost*
> O God, you poured down tongues of fire on the apostles at Pentecost.

All Saints Day
In the waters of the font, O God, you bind us together with the baptized saints of every time and place.

Another Sunday
In holy baptism, O God, you gather your people together to become bread for a hungry world.

As we joyfully anticipate the baptism of *name/s* (on *baptismal festival/day*), pour out your mercy extravagantly on *them*. May your holy angels keep watch over *them*, so that the wicked one may have no power over *them*.

Praying for the newly baptized during the Easter season:
Rejoicing in the glory of the resurrection, let us pray for *name/s, their sponsors/ godparents, their family*, and all those newly baptized into Christ across the globe. Continue to raise them up with your Spirit, feed them by your word, and empower them to be your hands in a broken world.

Praying for the newly baptized (and the community) the Sunday after a baptism has taken place:
For *name/s*, now sealed by the Holy Spirit and marked with the cross of Christ forever; for *their sponsors/godparents;* for *their families;* for this community of faith, and that we might find many ways to support *name/s* in *their* new life in Christ.

Making Disciples in Intercultural Settings

Have you ever walked into a cultural setting different from yours and found yourself totally at sea? "I have no idea what's going on!" is a common reaction. This can be profoundly unsettling, yet as our society continues to be increasingly pluralistic we are invited to navigate these deeper seas all the time.

You may have noticed that as human beings we do not live in the same way everywhere at all times. This phenomenon—the varieties of human ways of living—is what we mean by cultures. For example, gratitude exists in both India and Guatemala, but the way it is expressed varies. Anglos and Hispanics relate to time in different ways, and hospitality will be shown differently in a Native American household than in a Turkish one. It is wise to keep this in mind as our congregations increasingly include people of different cultural backgrounds, for perhaps the greatest challenge facing us today as communities is how to live together in justice, peace, and love, while respecting our diversity.

Honoring differences—and even learning from them—is crucial as we implement and lead a process of discipleship. Congregations invite inquirers to explore life in their communities, but there is no requirement that they stop being Turkish, Indian, Guatemalan, or Anglo, for that matter. A person's culture is not easily changed; its longevity across generations, migration, and other changes in life is impressive, even as a person grows and develops to become part of a culture other than her or his own.

Core Assumptions

Even in this sea of diversity, the core assumptions about making disciples transcend culture and are valid in all cultural settings. Some of these core assumptions are:

1. "Christians are made, not born," as Tertullian pointed out. God makes Christians who are accompanied and supported by the church through journeys toward becoming members of the faith community.

2. Making disciples involves conversion, understood as a change in the way we live our lives, and not only as intellectual assent to propositions.

3. The inquirer needs fellow travelers for support: a congregation, catechists, sponsors, and others, for though the journey is exciting it is also challenging.

4. Prayers (or rites) within a congregation's regular worship life accompany the progress and development along this journey of conversion.

5. Generally speaking, the catechumen hears the scriptures read and experiences worship, then reflects on them afterward, rather than learning about these things before experiencing them.

Although these five characteristics of making disciples are fairly universal, they are not lived out everywhere in the same ways. In many situations the catechists, sponsors, and congregation will belong predominantly to the same culture. In such situations the participants share the same cultural way of being in the world, and their ways of expression, values, style, even body language and sense of humor will be engaged naturally without need for translation or adaptation. In these cases the process of making disciples is incarnated in that cultural milieu naturally, even unconsciously.

Questions to Ask

In intercultural situations some questions arise if we are to incarnate making disciples in a cultural context different from our own:

- How do people learn, grow, and develop in this other culture?
- How do people share their experience with each other? Some cultures might see sharing as being too exposed to strangers or may have formalized forms of exchange.
- Does the culture have traditional ways of marking progress ritually?
- Do the roles of learner/explorer, catechist, sponsor, godparents, etc. already exist in the culture? How are these lived out?

The pastor, team leader, and catechists must be aware of these cultural differences, ready to learn from them and to make necessary adaptations. Otherwise the danger is that the culturally other inquirer will participate politely while remaining emotionally disengaged. Worse still, the inquirer might end up confusing Christianity with the dominant culture.

Spotting Cultural Difference

The process of being sensitive to other cultural backgrounds often begins with an experience of being at sea, but it is energized by our becoming aware of our own cultural envelope. Sometimes we become aware of cultural difference by its differentness.

For example, Annie, a catechist, invited Aurora, a 28-year-old inquirer, to read the gospel passage during a session. "I forgot my glasses," Aurora explained, embarrassed. Annie insisted, thinking Aurora just needed some support. Aurora could barely read, and remained stone silent during the rest of the session. In fact Annie had publicly embarrassed Aurora, who had finished school in Mexico only through the compulsory sixth grade.

Going home that night, Annie began to reflect upon what her expectations had been. "Wow," she thought, "I really blew it, all the time thinking I was trying to include Aurora. I guess I expected a 28-year-old to be able to read. Hmm. And I guess I also expected her to recover from the embarrassment more quickly, and to share more easily."

This anecdote brings up some assumptions that can often wreak havoc in intercultural situations:

- **"We are all the same,"** and **"One size fits all."** As human beings we have equal value—and rights—before God, but we do not live out our lives in the same way. Thus the very first challenge in an intercultural disciple making setting is to let go of the expectation that one size fits all or that everyone is the same.

- **"The leader should only facilitate."** Although this is a valuable goal, sometimes people from a different culture are nonplussed when someone in a leadership role acts in a non-directive way. "I don't know. What do you think?" may be a good way to facilitate conversation, but to a Latino or Latina, brought up instinctively to expect leaders and teachers to know something valuable, the speaker sounds lazy or ignorant.

- **"Anyone can interpret the Bible."** Again, this is true, but five hundred years of colonialism have created a tendency in members of colonized cultures, as well as the poor everywhere, to internalize oppression. Members of these cultures may assume they know nothing or remain silent while respectfully expecting truth to be doled out by teachers. Do not be surprised if it takes longer to loosen the voices of inquirers (and sponsors) of a different cultural background, but do not give up. Above all, do not be afraid to say privately at an informal moment, "Gee, I was hoping you'd share your experience with us—we are eager to hear what you have to say. The shy *other* expects your leadership and permission in order to participate.

- **"We'll make it up as we go along."** While many a catechist might be creative and enjoy flying by the seat of her pants with nothing more than the lectionary, many participants from other cultures expect clear training, resources, and supportive supervision. This is an important aspect of the ministry of both the pastor and team leader. Catechists, inquirers, and sponsors may be eager to participate, but they do expect the leaders to lead. Do not be afraid to explain how to participate and to supply resources and examples. Emotional support ("You are doing a great job!") is essential, but it is not enough. Participants expect and have a right to receive a general map and a sense of the process through which discipleship making takes place. Approaching participants with something like, "Oh, we just hang out as friends and share," can be heard as, "You are too stupid to understand what we are doing." Or, "I have no idea how to do this." Not good.

Countering the Culture—From Within

All seekers are invited to a new culture that is the Christian way of life, something that will challenge whatever culture a person is from. In the kingdom of God, children and those who are poor or sick are most important. Life in the kingdom of God is a way of life profoundly counter to worldly cultures that are shaped by love of control, money, and self-importance. The Christian way of life challenges all cultures.

Therefore it is not surprising that an inquirer may have to face some of her own culture's assumptions and challenge them. If the inquirer begins to identify these, it is also dangerously easy for her to replace them with Anglo cultural assumptions, which could mean that she would then be embarking in a journey of conversion to Anglo culture rather than the culture of the kingdom of God. Instead, the inquirer is invited to become a member of a community that is called to live by values that are profoundly different from those of all human cultural envelopes. God does not make a Native American Christian by teaching him how to be Spanish; rather, within his Native American culture, if he is to follow the way of Jesus Christ, he is invited to question and challenge it.

Conclusion

Christians are made, yes, but they are made within a culture. In order to support this process, discipleship teams must:

- be aware of their own cultural envelope,
- become aware of the cultural envelopes of the participants,
- notice how the cultural envelopes differ, and
- be flexible enough to honor and include different ways of doing things in the range of interactions that characterize the disciple making process.

This requires a high degree of flexibility and humility as well as a low need for control. In this way, as they reflect upon God's great deeds in their own lives, participants from different cultures will be able to hear and appreciate them in their own cultural ways, evidencing the presence of the Spirit: "Parthians, Medes, Elamites, and residents of Mesopotamia, Judea and Cappadocia, Pontus and Asia, Phrygia and Pamphylia, Egypt and the parts of Libya belonging to Cyrene, and visitors from Rome, both Jews and proselytes, Cretans and Arabs—in our own languages we hear them speaking about God's deeds of power" (Acts 2:9-11).

Adapting the Process of Making Disciples to Your Congregation

A chaplain borrows a bedpan from the nurse's station, fills it at the sink and uses the water to baptize a man who is on his deathbed. A congregation gathers at the river to baptize some new converts by total immersion. A pastor wipes tears from the face of a grieving mother and with them baptizes her newborn who will not survive the day. By these and a multitude of other ways, people have been initiated into life in Christ. The church has shown great flexibility and imagination at a central point in its life, holy baptism.

The key to making disciples in your congregation is to claim that same flexibility and imagination. Every congregation will shape this process to fit its own gifts and needs. If your congregation has a discipleship team of twenty, great! They can provide meals at every gathering, have three or four lay catechists, and break into multiple small groups. If your congregation has twenty at worship, great! You can have a meal or not, have the pastor be the catechist (inviting a lay person to apprentice the first time through), and do what you can do without worrying about what you cannot do. Suggestions for best practices are just that, suggestions. You might want to work toward them, but do not let them restrain you from jumping in.

The process described in this book provides an order: inquiry, exploration, intense preparation, and baptismal living. These form the latticework on which each congregation makes its own process. Several sample formats are provided in this handbook. Look at them, but keep your specific congregation in mind. Is music a gift at your church? Use hymnody to introduce the faith. Art? Use the visual arts to help people see images of faith. Trusting relationships? Channel these toward the intentional formation of disciples. Whatever the gifts of the congregation happen to be, bring them to the process of making disciples.

Those of us in congregations that are used to tight budgets may flinch, but the process of making disciples should encourage the congregation toward extravagance. Think of the parable of the one lost sheep. If just one person comes to your congregation to explore the faith or join your fellowship, do for one person what you would do for a dozen. All of the formation and all of the worship resources that you might offer to a large group should not be denied a single individual. Dare to make the welcome and accompaniment of one as rich and deep as for many. Of course it will not be only for one person, since that individual may be in a good position to invite other non-churched friends in the future. Besides, the catechist, the sponsor, the seeker, and the entire congregation will experience the blessings of renewal. Be extravagant with time, welcome, prayer, formation, and imagination. It did not take one congregation much money at all to go from using a small baptismal bowl to having an indoor waterfall ending in a baptismal pool. It took just one phone call to a landscape fountain contractor who loved the idea. He was full of suggestions and gave freely of his expertise to create a beautiful, temporary space in which to baptize. Think extravagantly, that is to say with imagination. God will provide.

Indeed, God has provided. Every congregation already has what it needs to make the process of making a disciples a rich and life-giving experience. In every congregation the Spirit has gathered people of prayer, people who yearn to share their love of God, and people whose lives are models of the godly life. In every congregation there are rich relationships and creative people. These are the most important gifts. With these gifts, a structure to follow, and lots of imagination, your congregation will create a powerful way for people to come to know Jesus.

Cata-What?
A Brief History of the Catechumenate

PERSECUTIONS

Especially from the second century on, emperors called for persecutions of Christians out of fear that the gods would not be favorable to the empire unless there was true devotion to the gods of the empire among all. Becoming disciples of Jesus in the early church meant becoming a part of a people who could face persecution and possibly martyrdom.

MARTYRDOM

The martyrs were the highest evidence of Christian living. The martyrs lived to die and died to live in Christ.

THE CATECHUMENATE BEGINS

With the martyrs as models of faithful living in their life and death, Christians took seriously the transformation expected of individuals who wished to become Christian. To prepare for this transformed life, the early church welcomed adult newcomers into the Christian faith by gradually introducing them to a life of discipleship over the course of several months or even years through sponsorship and participation in worship and study of scripture.

ONE UNIFIED RITE

In the early church (and in the Eastern Orthodox Church still today) baptism, anointing with oil, the laying on of hands, and admission to holy communion all happened at the same time.

CONSTANTINE'S EDICT

In the year 313 the Emperor Constantine announced that Christianity would be tolerated, and the number of individuals attracted to the Christian life rose.

INFANT BAPTISM

After Constantine's edict, Christianity became the state religion and adult baptism became less the norm. Children were being brought up in Christian homes and infant baptisms became preeminent.

SEPARATION OF RITES

During the medieval era in the West local priests would baptize children, and when the bishop was available he would confirm the baptism through the laying on of hands. This separate occasion later became a rite of confirmation unto itself and first communion did not occur until after confirmation.

RE-ROOTING CHRISTIANITY

During the Reformation era, confirmation—typically in early adolescence, followed by reception of holy communion—became an opportunity for learning about the Bible and traditions of the church through catechisms.

RECOVERY OF THE CATECHUMENATE

From the sixteenth through the nineteenth centuries, there is evidence of Roman Catholic missionaries having recovered the catechumenate for adult conversion accompanying colonization in Latin America, India, and Africa.

BAPTISM, FIRST HOLY COMMUNION, CONFIRMATION

During the twentieth century, conversations about the importance of receiving holy communion at a younger age led Roman Catholics and eventually many Protestants to flip the rites of first holy communion and confirmation. Common practice is now for infants to be baptized, receive first communion when the child is ready as determined by the parents, the pastor, and congregational practice, and then be confirmed during adolescence.

RITE OF CHRISTIAN INITIATION OF ADULTS (RCIA)

Also during the twentieth century, the Roman Catholic Church developed a staged process for receiving adults through baptism. RCIA incorporates a similar process for receiving people from other traditions into the full communion of the Roman Catholic Church.

PROTESTANTS RECOVER THE CATECHUMENATE

Mutual conversation between the Roman Catholic and many Protestant denominations led to the development of materials encouraging Protestant congregations to welcome the unbaptized to Christ through the catechumenate, and in some instances adapt the process to affirm the faith of previously baptized Christians.

ONE UNIFIED RITE AGAIN

In most cases newly baptized adults will receive the anointing with oil, laying on of hands, and holy communion all at the same time.

THE CATECHUMENATE TODAY

Inquirers and affirmers gather with congregational members to practice together what it means to be disciples of Jesus Christ, regularly reading scripture, praying, worshiping, and serving.

Forming Christians, Transforming Congregations

The assumptions we make always play a major role in shaping how we welcome people into Christian community. Take, for example, the story of how the disciple making process emerged in the life of the early church. In the first centuries after Christ's death and resurrection, church leaders assumed that dying and rising was the essence of our life in Christ. They remembered the apostle Paul's declaration that "if anyone is in Christ, there is a new creation: everything old has passed away; see, everything has become new!" (2 Cor. 5:17). They were also drawn to Paul's understanding of baptism as a journey from death into life. "Do you not know," Paul wrote, "that all of us who have been baptized into Christ Jesus were baptized into his death? Therefore we have been buried with him by baptism into death, so that, just as Christ was raised from the dead by the glory of the Father, so we too might walk in newness of life" (Rom. 6:3-4). Not surprisingly, the process of welcoming people into Christian community in the early church mirrored this image of transformation and renewal. From one community to another the process was one of conversion into which every person was called, without regard to race, gender, status, age, social class, or religious identity.

Another basic assumption of early church leaders was that all those welcomed into Christian community needed to be formed in faith. Jesus had commissioned his followers to go and make disciples of all nations by baptizing them and by teaching them to observe all that he had commanded (Matt. 28:19-20). Here again, no one was excluded. As the early church father Tertullian observed, "Christians are made, not born" (*Apologeticus*, xviii). With that view in mind, those who developed an early catechumenal process allowed ample time for all participants to hear God's word together and to learn the meaning of living in the way of Christ.

A third very important assumption of early church leaders was that the radical way of Christ was seldom aligned with mainstream cultural values. The whole notion of a Christian culture or a Christian nation had yet to emerge, so a process of making disciples was focused on strengthening and equipping Christ's followers for daily living in ways that made them bold and resilient to the challenges they faced.

Assumptions of a (Recently) Churched Culture

The assumptions and practices of the early church contrast significantly with the assumptions made by many church leaders in North America in the past century.

Those assumptions also played a major role in shaping how we welcomed people into our respective communities. First, we widely assumed that newcomers were more in need of information than conversion. Since the culture in which people were raised was presumably Christian, we focused on teaching people about the uniqueness of our particular denominations and about the important theological perspectives that have shaped our way of understanding the Christian faith. In mainline Protestant congregations, this was typically done in a new member class that lasted for a few weeks.

Secondly, it was widely assumed that most newcomers were already acquainted with the Bible and with the basic language of the Christian faith. If they had been raised in a family that attended church even occasionally, we assumed they were *born* Christian and that they came to us already formed in some way. The process of welcome seldom anticipated primary questions of faith such as "Who is Jesus?" or "How is the Bible God's word?"

Finally, we accepted the common assumption that we lived in a "Christian nation" with mainstream cultural values rooted in the teachings of Jesus. As we welcomed people into Christian community we focused very little on the process of strengthening and equipping people to be bold and resilient against the powerful forces of individualism, consumerism, and a whole host of other societal pressures that lured them away from their baptismal callings.

Regrettably, nearly every mainline Protestant denomination in North America experienced a steep decline in membership during the past few decades. The reasons for this decline are many and complex. One clear consequence of this crisis is that it has challenged nearly every assumption we made in the years preceding the decline, and that has led many of us into a process of transformation and renewal that feels very much like dying and rising with Christ. As new life emerges in Christian communities across the continent we are discovering that the assumptions made by early church leaders remain true in every time and place.

Transforming the Church of Today

So what does it look like when Christian communities of the twenty-first century allow first-century assumptions to shape our process of welcoming people? First, we reclaim the notions that dying and rising is the very essence of our life in Christ and that all people, without distinction, are in need of conversion. From that perspective, we can also structure a process of welcome that invites people into a journey of faith that immerses them in the waters of baptism. Instead of calling this a *new member class*, we sometimes use terms such as "The Way" or "Faith Journey," which help us move the focus from information to transformation. Then we walk with people through the four stages of the disciple making process that are described in this handbook, adapting each stage to the unique culture and contexts of our particular place.

Second, Christian communities are reclaiming the notion that "Christians are made, not born." Faith formation is at the heart of the welcoming process from beginning to end. All assumptions about what people know and don't know about the Bible are cast aside, along with false expectations that everyone will somehow know the basic language of the Christian faith. We consciously try not to move too quickly. Whereas a typical new member class might last for just a few weeks, communities using an intentional disciple making process (based on an ancient and revived model of the catechumenate) often take anywhere from three months to one year in order to allow ample time for hearing God's word together and going deeper into the question of what it means to live in the way of Christ. Some have said that the curriculum for this time of faith formation is simply lectionary and life.

Third, guided by the assumption that the way of Christ is seldom aligned with mainstream cultural values, communities using a disciple making process today are also creating a safe space for people to come to terms with this reality and to find forgiveness, hope, and strength in their daily efforts to renounce the societal pressures and the powers of this world that rebel against God. In the end, not only the people being welcomed in this way are experiencing transformation, but stories abound that relate how the whole community gets caught up in this holy work of God. Wading into the waters of baptism together, all are reminded that dying and rising is the essence of our life in Christ, that faith formation is a lifelong process, and that the call to discipleship is not only challenging but deeply rewarding.

Dates for Easter and Related Days

LECTIONARY	YEAR	ASH WEDNESDAY	EASTER	PENTECOST
B	2012	February 22	April 8	May 27
C	2013	February 13	March 31	May 19
A	2014	March 5	April 20	June 8
B	2015	February 18	April 5	May 24
C	2016	February 10	March 27	May 15
A	2017	March 1	April 16	June 4
B	2018	February 14	April 1	May 20
C	2019	March 6	April 21	June 9
A	2020	February 26	April 12	May 31
B	2021	February 17	April 4	May 23
C	2022	March 2	April 17	June 5
A	2023	February 22	April 9	May 28
B	2024	February 14	March 31	May 19
C	2025	March 5	April 20	June 8
A	2026	February 18	April 5	May 24
B	2027	February 10	March 28	May 16
C	2028	March 1	April 16	June 4
A	2029	February 14	April 1	May 20
B	2030	March 6	April 21	June 9
C	2031	February 26	April 13	June 1
A	2032	February 11	March 28	May 16
B	2033	March 2	April 17	June 5
C	2034	February 22	April 9	May 28
A	2035	February 7	March 25	May 13
B	2036	February 27	April 13	June 1
C	2037	February 18	April 5	May 24
A	2038	March 10	April 25	June 13
B	2039	February 23	April 10	May 29
C	2040	February 15	April 1	May 20

CONTRIBUTORS

Daniel Benedict, OSL, writes and teaches in the arenas of liturgy and spirituality, including the catechumenal process. He is abbot of the Order of Saint Luke and a presbyter (elder) in the United Methodist Church. He lives in Hawaii.

Dennis Bushkofsky is a pastor of the Evangelical Lutheran Church in America who has led adults to baptism and contributed to published resources used in making disciples for over twenty years. He serves as an interim pastor in the Chicago area.

Kirsty DePree served the Reformed Church in America as coordinator of discipleship for five years. She serves as minister of discipleship at Marble Collegiate Church in New York City.

Jessicah Krey Duckworth is a practical theologian whose research lies at the intersections of Christian formation, intercultural and multigenerational care practices, and newcomer participation in congregations. She teaches congregational and community care at Luther Seminary in St. Paul, Minnesota, and is ordained in the Evangelical Lutheran Church in America.

Bryon Hansen is pastor at Bethlehem Lutheran Church in Auburn, California. He is a practitioner of the catechumenate, past board member of the North American Association for the Catechumenate, and involved in the catechumenate team of the Sierra Pacific Synod of the Evangelical Lutheran Church in America.

John W. B. Hill is a presbyter of the Anglican diocese of Toronto and author of *Making Disciples: Serving Those Who Are Entering the Christian Life*. His passion is helping cultivate liturgical competencies.

Jay Koyle is a presbyter in the Anglican Church of Canada. He serves as congregational development officer for the Diocese of Algoma, after many years' experience as a parish pastor, professor of theology, and catechumenal practitioner. He is president of The Associated Parishes for Liturgy and Mission, director of Table Song: Eighth Day Perspectives, and a board member of the North American Association for the Catechumenate.

Dirk G. Lange's ministerial experience has covered a wide spectrum of activities, but all under one umbrella: liturgy in the lives of people. As a brother of Taizé, he was engaged with the prayer and songs of Taizé working closely with the composer. Dirk is associate professor of worship at Luther Seminary, St. Paul, Minnesota. He has served parishes in Atlanta and Philadelphia.

Charles E. Mantey is pastor at Saint Mark Lutheran Church in Salem, Oregon. He has been actively involved in the catechumenal process over the past five years in two congregations and has helped lead catechumenal training events for congregations in the Northwest United States.

Michael Merriman is one of the first practitioners of the catechumenal process in the Episcopal Church. He serves on the staff of the Episcopal Church of the Transfiguration in Dallas, Texas, primarily in adult Christian formation.

Juan M. C. Oliver, an Episcopal priest, is the former director of the Hispanic Program at the General Seminary in New York and author of *Ripe Fields: The Promise and Challenge of Latino Ministry.*

Paul Palumbo is pastor at Lake Chelan Lutheran Church in Chelan, Washington. The catechumenate has been central to his parish ministry for nearly two decades.

Mary E. Peterson is a pastor in the Evangelical Lutheran Church in America who serves as a hospice chaplain. She lives in Portland, Oregon, and is also a spiritual director as well as a retreat leader.

Rick Rouse is the director of the Missional Leadership Academy for the Grand Canyon Synod of the Evangelical Lutheran Church in America and president of the North American Association for the Catechumenate. He has served as parish pastor, teacher, conference speaker, and church consultant, and is the author of two books published by Augsburg Fortress.

Jan Ruud is a Lutheran parish pastor in Tacoma, Washington. He was introduced to the adult catechumenate while serving as a missionary in Cameroon and has used this process in congregations within the United States for the last twenty years.

Craig A. Satterlee, an Evangelical Lutheran Church in America pastor, teaches preaching at the Lutheran School of Theology at Chicago and University of Notre Dame. Craig writes and speaks about the relationship of worship and preaching and areas of congregational life and mission.

Teresa Stricklen is the associate for worship in the Office of Theology and Worship for the Presbyterian Church (USA).

Mons Teig is emeritus professor of worship at Luther Seminary in St. Paul, Minnesota. Previously he was director for worship and preaching in the former American Lutheran Church and a pastor in Brooklyn, New York, and Pacific Palisades, California.

ACKNOWLEDGMENTS

"This life, therefore…" quote is from Martin Luther, "Defense and Explanation of All the Articles," *Luther's Works,* vol. 32, *Career of the Reformer II* (Philadelphia: Fortress Press, 1958), 24.

"The missional church…" quote is from Rick Rouse and Craig Van Gelder, *A Field Guide for the Missional Congregation: Embarking on a Journey of Transformation* (Minneapolis: Augsburg Fortress, 2008), 23-24.

"The borderland church…" quote is from Gary Nelson, *Borderland Churches: A Congregation's Introduction to Missional Living* (St. Louis: Chalice Press, 2008), 132.

"Discipleship is all about…" quote is from Rick Rouse and Craig Van Gelder, *A Field Guide for the Missional Congregation: Embarking on a Journey of Transformation* (Minneapolis: Augsburg Fortress, 2008), 65.

The section on Leadership Skills is from a paper written by pioneer catechumenal process practitioners Tom and Ann McElligott and used here with their permission. Copyright © Tom and Ann McElligott. Revised 1997.

"My Life Story" and "My Story" are story sharing exercises in use by Phinney Ridge Lutheran Church in Seattle, Washington.

Martin Luther's Four-Stranded Garland is based on his instruction on how to pray the Ten Commandments from "A Simple Way to Pray," *Luther's Works*, vol. 43, *Devotional Writings II* (Philadelphia: Fortress Press, 1968), 193-211. Adapted by Jim Christanson, Stewart McDonald, and Dennis Bushkofsky.

Small group blessings and prayers are from *Welcome to Christ: A Lutheran Catechetical Guide* (Minneapolis: Augsburg Fortress, 1997).

"A Word to Preachers" is adapted from D. Jay Koyle, *Calling the Church to Its Heart: Preaching, Parish Catechumenate, and the Revitalization of the Twenty-first Century Congregation* (Chicago: Seabury-Western, 2008).

"The light of the sacraments be inculcated in the candidates as surprise" quote is from Craig A. Satterlee in *Ambrose of Milan's Method of Mystagogical Preaching* (Collegeville, Minnesota: Pueblo, 2002), 318.

"Explaining rites can easily lapse…" quote is from William Harmless, s.j., *Augustine and the Catechumenate* (Collegeville, Minnesota: Pueblo, 1995), 365.

"Constructing a Temporary Font" is from Dennis L. Bushkofsky and Craig A. Satterlee, *Using Evangelical Lutheran Worship*, vol. 2, "The Christian Life: Baptism and Life Passages" (Minneapolis: Augsburg Fortress, 2008), 42-43.

"Praying for Those Preparing for Baptism and the Newly Baptized" has been adapted from *Washed and Welcome: A Baptism Sourcebook* (Minneapolis: Augsburg Fortress, 2010).

GLOSSARY

Affirmation of Baptism—A rite for already baptized older youth or adults that typically follows an extended process of instruction and faith formation. In some denominational traditions this may also incorporate or be variously known as *confirmation, reception, reaffirmation,* or *reconciliation.* In most cases this book refers to all of these possibilities within the framework of affirmation of baptism. In this book, people who are preparing for affirmation of baptism are typically referred to as *affirmation candidates* or *affirmers.*

Affirmation of Vocation—A public blessing and prayer occurring in the congregation's worship to inaugurate and sustain a person's Christian identity through one or more daily life settings. Some congregations use such a rite as a culmination of the period of baptismal living, a few weeks following baptism or affirmation of baptism. If baptism or affirmation of baptism occurred at the Vigil of Easter, an affirmation of vocation might occur on the Day of Pentecost.

Assisting minister—A lay worship leader (in some traditions known as a deacon) who may lead prayers of intercession as well as other prayers, prepare the altar with the elements for communion, participate in distribution of communion, dismiss the worshiping assembly, and serve as a reader for one or more passages of scripture. An assisting minister may have a particular role during rites in the disciple making process.

Baptism—A sacrament of spiritual rebirth through water and the Holy Spirit, wherein the triune God delivers a person from the powers of sin and death, giving new life in Jesus Christ. Baptism marks a person's incorporation into the universal church as well as into a particular congregation. While baptism might occur at any time, ordinarily it is within a regular service of a congregation. Since the ancient church, the paradigmatic moment for adult baptism in particular has been at the Vigil of Easter. For a few weeks after baptism (particularly throughout the fifty-day season of Easter if baptism was at the Vigil of Easter) candidates are typically called the newly baptized (or *neophytes* in some traditions).

Baptismal Covenant—Commitment to the church's teachings, disciplines, and service through a brief set of formal questions that is a part of the baptismal liturgy, also used with those affirming their baptism and with the entire worshiping assembly, especially on baptismal festivals (Vigil of Easter, Day of Pentecost, All Saints Day, and the Baptism of Our Lord). Even though not every tradition has a baptismal covenant as such, most candidates for baptism or affirmation of baptism indicate their commitment to Christ and the church through assent to one or more questions or vows.

Baptismal Living—The period after baptism. During this period new or returning Christians engage in reflection, embracing and entering into baptismal living by means of guided and sustained contemplation of the church's worship, especially baptism and communion, using biblical themes, images, and narratives. Technically the period continues throughout all of life following baptism, although in a more narrow sense it may refer to a period of time following baptism when the newly baptized are encouraged to reflect on their experiences of receiving the sacraments and being received into the full communion of the church. Sometimes this period is also known as *mystagogy*. This period often culminates with an affirmation of vocation that might occur on the Day of Pentecost. See also *mystagogical reflection*.

Candidate—A person preparing for baptism may be called a *baptismal candidate* after having been enrolled for baptism. Affirmation of baptism candidates (an *affirmation candidate* or an *affirmer* or *reaffirmer*) might be so identified at any point after they have expressed a desire to affirm baptism. Some traditions call those who have been enrolled for baptism the *elect*.

Catechesis—The explicit formation of persons into Christian faith and life. It includes various modes of instruction, reflection on the scriptures and church teachings, as well as an apprenticeship in prayer, worship, and service in the world. It is a lifelong process and the responsibility of the congregation and its leaders. A person who has already received some type of formation may be described as being *catechized*. In some traditions catechesis also involves the teaching and learning of catechisms.

Catechist—A person who guides people in their faith formation. A catechist designs and leads disciple making sessions and encourages newcomers in their practices of worship, reflection on scripture, prayer, and service.

Catechumen—An unbaptized inquirer publicly welcomed by the congregation (usually during a *rite of welcome*) and encouraged to encounter Jesus Christ, hear the word of God, pray, and participate in the ministry of a local congregation.

Catechumenate—A process that prepares adults for baptism by facilitating their participation in the practices of Christian discipleship and publicly marking their participation within the body of Christ through rites of *welcome*, *enrollment*, and *baptism* (also in some cases an *affirmation of vocation*). Frequently the phrase *catechumenal process* is used to refer to parallel processes that prepare already baptized persons for affirmation of baptism, reaffirmation of baptism, or reconciliation with the church.

Christian Discipleship—The pattern of life lived and described by Jesus Christ.

Christian Initiation—see *Baptism*.

Confirmation—Historically, a prayer for receiving the gifts of the Holy Spirit at baptism, often spoken by a bishop. From the Middle Ages onward in the Christian West, confirmation has usually been experienced as a separate rite from baptism, in many cases still performed by bishops (particularly in the Roman Catholic and Anglican/Episcopal traditions), after a period of instruction and faith formation. See also *Affirmation of Baptism*.

Disciple—A follower or adherent of Jesus Christ.

Enrollment, Rite of—A public blessing and prayer service occurring in the congregation's worship to mark a catechumen's intention to be baptized within a few weeks. When baptism will be at the Vigil of Easter, a rite of enrollment will often occur on the first Sunday in Lent. If baptism is on the Baptism of Our Lord (a Sunday in early January), a rite of enrollment will often occur at the beginning of Advent. The rite of enrollment formally concludes the exploration stage for a catechumen and begins the stage of intense preparation. After enrollment the catechumen is typically called a *baptismal candidate* (in the Roman Catholic tradition such candidates are usually referred to as the *elect*). Although candidates for affirmation of baptism might also be identified in parallel rites at this time, since they have already been baptized they do not need to enroll for that sacrament.

Exploration—A period of time following inquiry when catechumens and affirmation candidates participate actively in the practices of Christian discipleship alongside catechists and sponsors.

Formation—The ongoing activity of the Holy Spirit giving shape to the faith of a person, particularly a lifelong process of participating in the practices of a Christian community.

Inquirer—A person who has indicated initial interest in a Christian congregation. Such a person may have been baptized or not, but is interested in exploring broad and general questions about faith and Christianity as a religion. If an inquirer has already been baptized, such a person has indicated an interest in returning to a life of faith or participating in a new congregation.

Inquiry—An initial period of time when inquirers explore broad and general questions about faith and Christianity alongside catechists and sponsors.

Intense Preparation—A period of time, often during the season of Lent, when candidates for baptism or affirmation of baptism focus their preparation for baptism through reflection on the creeds, the prayer and worship life of the church, the baptismal covenant, and practices of Christian discipleship. Catechists and sponsors continue to play important roles as companions. This period concludes with baptism or affirmation of baptism, often at the Vigil of Easter.

Lectionary—A set of three scripture readings and a psalm appointed for each Sunday and major festival of the liturgical year. Ordinarily a first reading from the Old Testament (in Easter from the book of Acts), a psalm (often sung or spoken in recitation format), a New Testament reading (often from a letter from one of the apostles), and a gospel reading. The Revised Common Lectionary is a three-year system of readings (years A, B, and C) used by many denominations and that also relates closely to the Roman Catholic Church's Lectionary for Mass.

Making Disciples—The phrase adopted by this book and other resources to refer to a staged process of inviting and preparing adult candidates for baptism, affirmation of baptism, or reaffirmation of baptism. It incorporates what many have also termed the *catechumenate* or the *catechumenal process*.

Means of Grace—In broad terms these are any channels that God uses to communicate with people, but particularly through the sacraments of Holy Baptism and Holy Communion, and through reading and preaching the divine word of God.

Mystagogical reflection—This is a time of settling in to the new reality of being a Christian. Catechists, pastors, and others who guide the newly baptized in the early days of this transition help them to reflect on their recent experiences of receiving the sacraments of baptism and the eucharist (the *mysteries*) and to draw upon those gifts for their daily lives of faith.

Mystagogy—See *Baptismal Living*.

Newcomer—See *Inquirer*.

Newly baptized—A recently baptized Christian who is encouraged to explore meaning around the sacraments of Holy Baptism and Holy Communion and the implications for living as a disciple of Jesus Christ in daily life. In some traditions this person is called a *neophyte*.

Paschal (Easter) candle—The candle lit from the new fire at the Vigil of Easter. The paschal candle is lit through the fifty days of Easter and at every Christian baptism and funeral in order to connect the promise of Christ's new life given through baptism to each disciple.

Paschal mystery—Paschal means Easter. The paschal mystery recalls Christ's passing from death to life, as well as the ancient Hebrew people's passage from slavery in Egypt to freedom in the promised land. The paschal mystery of faith is that through baptism Christians are joined to the suffering, death, and resurrection of Jesus Christ through whom God brings people to faith and new life.

Pastor—The pastor of a disciple making congregation publicly supports the process by serving as a spiritual director and a guide to catechists, and by empowering the ministries of others. This resource often uses *presiding minister* to indicate the liturgical role that pastors and priests often perform publicly in the process of making disciples. Various traditions might also refer to this liturgical role as a *celebrant* or a *presiding minister*.

Presiding minister—See *Pastor*.

Reaffirmation or **Reaffirmers**—See *Affirmation of Baptism*.

Reception—See *Affirmation of Baptism*.

Reconciliation—See *Affirmation of Baptism*.

Rite of Christian Initiation of Adults (RCIA)—The process for receiving adults into the Roman Catholic Church, either through baptism (the catechumenate) or through parallel processes of reception into full communion.

Seeker—See *Inquirer*.

Sponsor—A Christian who accompanies newcomers on their journey towards baptism and lifelong discipleship, sharing their encounters with Jesus Christ and their practices of Christian discipleship. Sponsors might also accompany returning members or people seeking to (re)affirm their baptism in a local congregation.

Team leader—A Christian who leads in recruiting the disciple making team and serves as the liaison between the team and other congregational leaders, especially the pastor. This person represents the process of making disciples to the congregation and often takes a significant role in the public rites as the person who presents candidates to the congregation.

Three Days, The—The church's worship for the days at the end of Holy Week marking Jesus Christ's passion, death, burial, and resurrection as told through the gospel accounts. Also called the *Triduum*.

> **Maundy Thursday** *(Holy Thursday)*—The day during Holy Week marking the night Jesus shared the Last Supper with his disciples and washed their feet.

> **Good Friday**—The day during Holy Week marking the suffering, death, and burial of Jesus.

> **Resurrection of Our Lord** (including the *Vigil of Easter* and *Easter Day*)—The day celebrating the resurrection of Jesus (marked from sunset on Holy Saturday through sunset on Easter Day).

> **Vigil of Easter**—Worship at a Vigil of Easter (anytime from sundown during the evening before Easter Day through sunrise on Easter morning) contains four movements: 1) the lighting of a paschal (Easter) candle from a new fire; 2) several scripture readings from the Old Testament that recall the history of salvation and anticipate God's ultimate saving act in Jesus Christ, a reading from one of the New Testament letters, and a gospel reading proclaiming the resurrection; 3) the celebration of baptism and/or affirmation of baptism; and 4) the celebration of the first eucharist of Easter.

Welcome, Rite of—A public blessing and prayer service marking the inquirers' intentions to begin a process of formation into the Christian faith. The welcome rite formally concludes the inquiry stage of making disciples. After this rite an unbaptized inquirer is typically called a *catechumen*, while an inquirer who is already baptized may be called an *affirmation candidate* or a *(re)affirmer*.

BIBLIOGRAPHY

Bible/Lectionary

The **Bible** is the basic resource for all disciples' growth, corporately and individually. Some resources that are useful to consider for the process of making disciples include:

Access Bible, updated edition (NRSV). Published by Oxford University Press, its explanations about challenging passages, words, and phrases may be particularly helpful for beginning readers of the Bible.

Common English Bible (CEB). A fresh, very readable contemporary English translation that has the support of several major mainline Christian denominations.

Revised Common Lectionary. A resource that provides a pattern for scripture readings for several Christian denominations throughout the world on each Sunday and major festival. Many denominational publishers have produced variations of the Revised Common Lectionary for use by the congregations they serve. A major online source for the Revised Common Lectionary is http://lectionary.library.vanderbilt.edu/.

Worship

Denominational worship book. The worship book (hymnals and prayer books as well) of the congregation is a central resource for corporate worship life in addition to providing help with private devotions.

Haas, David. **Who Calls You By Name: Music for Christian Initiation.** 2 vols. GIA. Music is provided in this collection for rites of welcome, enrollment, Vigil of Easter, Lenten blessings, presentations, and more. Also provides dramatizations with sung congregational responses for key readings from John during year A of the lectionary.

Hospitality

Homan, Father Daniel, OSB., and Lonni Collins Pratt. **Radical Hospitality.** Brewster, Massachusetts: Paraclete Press, 2002. Accessible little book about Benedictine hospitality, applicable to all Christians, but especially to those called to disciple making ministries.

Morris, Clay L. **Holy Hospitality: Worship and the Baptismal Covenant.** New York: Church Publishing, 2005. Helps churches think about hospitality as a reflection of God's invitation to all people. Considers liturgical space and the training of the laity to issue the welcome of Christ to everyone.

Christian Living in Vocation, Witness, and Service

The local congregation will have resources and activities in which candidates may participate in ongoing Christian education, worship, and service. Sponsors will be a major resource as they talk about Christian living, engage in service opportunities, and think together about the opportunities for witness and service as persons baptized into the mission of God in Christ Jesus.

Resources regarding ministry in daily life include:

Schwab, A. Wayne. ***When the Members Are the Missionaries: An Extraordinary Calling for Ordinary People.*** Hinesburg, Vermont: Member Mission Press, 2002. Helps people to identify the ways that they may serve God's mission through their daily life settings.

Schwab, A. Wayne, and Elizabeth S. Hall. ***Living the Gospel: A Guide for Individuals and Small Groups.*** A workbook available from www.membermission.org providing a way for people to discern how God is calling them in their homes, church, community, and wider world.

Van Gelder, Craig. ***The Ministry of the Missional Church.*** Grand Rapids: Baker, 2007. Parts of this book can help new members become leaders in a Spirit-led church.

Inquiry: Helpful Books to Recommend Based on Seekers' Questions

Boulding, Maria. ***Gateway to Resurrection.***
Lamott, Anne. ***Traveling Mercies*** and ***Plan B.***
Lewis, C. S. ***Mere Christianity.***
Miller, Donald. ***Blue Like Jazz.***
Winn, Albert Curry. ***A Christian Primer.***
Winner, Lauren. ***Girl Meets God.***

Resources for Implementing and Sustaining the Disciple Making Process

Ball, Peter, and Malcolm Grundy. ***Faith on The Way.*** London: Mowbry, 2000. Written from an Anglican perspective, this is a good book for church leaders to read in order to consider starting a disciple making process. Includes an outline for church leaders' prayerful discussion of the issues.

Benedict, Daniel T. *Come to the Waters.* Nashville: Discipleship Resources, 1996. The United Methodist resource for the catechumenate that discusses each stage and offers rites for various people seeking baptism or baptismal renewal. Very helpful Protestant adaptation of the Roman Catholic Rite of Christian Initiation of Adults (RCIA).

Birmingham, Mary. *Year-Round Catechumenate.* Chicago: Liturgy Training Publications, 2003. Tailoring the catechumenate so that when people are ready to explore the faith, congregations can start the process for them right then without making them wait to fit into parish schedules or plans.

Bushkofsky, Dennis L., and Craig A. Satterlee. *The Christian Life: Baptism and Life Passages.* Minneapolis: Augsburg Fortress, 2008. Chapter 4, pages 79-95 provide a brief introduction to a Lutheran pattern of the catechumenate contained in the 2006 *Evangelical Lutheran Worship.*

Companions on the Way. Reformed Church in America, 2005. A resource for those leading the catechumenate with materials for the unchurched, those wishing to affirm or renew baptismal vows, and those bringing infants for baptism.

Galipeau, Jerry. *Apprenticed to Christ: Activities for Practicing the Catholic Way of Life.* World Library Publications, 2007. Following the church year, this book provides apprenticeship activities for one of each Sunday's readings in the three-year lectionary cycle.

Gallagher, Maureen. *The Art of Catechesis: What You Need to Be, Know and Do.* Mahway, New Jersey: Paulist Press, 1998. This book helps catechists pass on the faith tradition by giving them ways to reflect upon their own encounters with scripture and the church with its stories, prayers, rituals, sacraments, and lifestyle. It is a good reference book for catechists in that it provides suggestions for activities as well as basic teaching.

Hill, John W. B. *Making Disciples: Serving Those Who Are Entering The Christian Life.* Toronto: The Hoskin Group/Anglican Book Centre, 1991.

Hixon, Barbara. *RCIA Spirituality.* Rev. ed. San Jose: Resource Publications, 1996. Excellent resource for disciple making teams to use for their own spiritual formation following the catechumenal process. Roman Catholic, easily adaptable for Protestants.

Hoffman, Paul E. *Faith Forming Faith: Bringing New Christians to Baptism and Beyond.* Eugene, Oregon: Wipf and Stock, 2012. Phinney Ridge Lutheran in Seattle discovered that by forming the faith of new Christians, they as a parish were renewed and revitalized for mission in the world.

Joncas, Jan Michael. *Preaching the Rites of Christian Initiation.* Chicago: Liturgy Training Publications, 1994. A Roman Catholic scholar gives guidance for preaching during the preparation of candidates for baptism and persons affirming their baptism.

Jones, Deborah. *The RCIA Journey: A Resource for the Catechumenate.* New London, Connecticut: Twenty-third Publications, 1997. A basic primer on the teachings of the Roman Catholic Church in 20 sessions with suggestions for scriptural, liturgical, reflective, and ethical engagement with these basic Christian themes and a closing prayer.

McElligott, Ann E. P. *The Catechumenal Process: Adult Initiation & Formation for Christian Life and Ministry.* New York: The Church Hymnal Corporation, 1990. This book details the implementation of the adult catechumenate and parallel rites for the baptized called for by the 1988 General Convention of the Episcopal Church.

Merriman, Michael W. *The Baptismal Mystery and the Catechumenate.* New York: The Church Hymnal Corporation, 1990. Essays by major liturgical theologians helpful for those interested in forming disciples. Looks at issues such as timing, the church's role, particular church members' roles, how catechesis differs from Christian education, the role of scripture, and vocation.

Mongoven, Anne Marie. *The Prophetic Spirit of Catechesis.* New York: Paulist Press, 2000. This book provides a way of doing catechesis through the symbols of the church.

Morris, Thomas H. *The RCIA: Transforming the Church.* New York: Paulist Press, 1989. This is a detailed description for implementation of the Rite of Christian Initiation of Adults (RCIA) for Roman Catholics. It also can provide insights as other denominations adapt this process to reflect their theology and practice.

North American Association for the Catechumenate (www.catechumenate.org) has many practical resources on its Web site. The organization also holds an annual training event that is helpful for disciple making leaders.

On the Way: Towards an Integrated Approach to Christian Initiation. London: The Central Board of Finance of the Church of England, 1995. This book asks many of the hard questions that any congregation might ask as they consider adopting this process of disciple making.

Ostdiek, Gilbert. *Catechesis for Liturgy.* Washington, D.C.: Pastoral Press, 1986. Focuses on attending to and reflecting upon our experience of liturgy in order to apply it to the disciple making process.

Ramshaw, Gail. *Words Around the Font.* Chicago: Liturgy Training Publications, 1994. Professor Ramshaw gives imaginative, insightful words that illumine the biblical texts used during the process of making disciples. Sponsors, candidates, and other leaders will be illumined by her images and insights.

Satterlee, Craig A., and Lester Ruth. *Creative Preaching on the Sacraments.* Nashville: Discipleship Resources, 2001. Two seminary professors, one a Methodist and the other a Lutheran, deal with preaching in the disciple making process.

Schattauer, Thomas H., editor. *Inside Out: Worship in an Age of Mission.* Minneapolis: Fortress Press, 1999. The whole book by Lutheran seminary professors stresses the mission dimension in worship. The chapter "Holy Baptism: Promise Big Enough for the World" provides a theological and practical basis for preparing seekers for baptism. It also stresses that it takes the whole church to raise the newly baptized.

Steffen, Donna, s.c. *Discerning Disciples: Listening for God's Voice in Christian Initiation.* New York: Paulist Press, 1997. Steffen emphasizes listening to the questions and issues of the baptismal candidates—an important part of the disciple making process—providing practical insights, examples, and questions that will help any sponsor or leader who works with seekers.

This Is the Night. Chicago: Liturgy Training Publications, 1992 (30 minutes, VHS). This is an inspirational video that intersperses liturgies with the response of candidates for baptism and reception of baptized persons into the Roman Catholic Church. Though it is no longer in print, the video's ability to capture the power of the formation process of the catechumenate as well as fully-embodied ritual is unmatched.

Wagner, Nick. *The Way of Faith: A Field Guide for the RCIA Process.* New London, Connecticut: Twenty-third Publications, 2008. This is an informal user-friendly book on the basics of the catechumenate written primarily for Roman Catholics, but could also be helpful for many Protestants.

Webber, Robert E. *Journey to Jesus: The Worship, Evangelism, and Nurture Mission of the Church.* Nashville: Abingdon, 2001. This book connects the missional nature of the church and its evangelism with the way of making disciples in the ancient church that translates into today's disciple making process.

Welcome to Christ booklets (5) and video. This series provides excellent resources that give guidance for the disciple making process plus specific liturgies that can be adapted by congregations to fit their specific context.

Welcome to Christ: A Lutheran Catechetical Guide. Minneapolis: Augsburg Fortress, 1997. A concise bibliography provides further resources on pages 52-54.

Welcome to Christ: A Lutheran Introduction to the Catechumenate. Minneapolis: Augsburg Fortress, 1997. A brief annotated bibliography is provided on pages 62-70.

Welcome to Christ: Lutheran Rites for the Catechumenate. Minneapolis: Augsburg Fortress, 1997. Music and liturgies are provided for the whole disciple making process.

Welcome to Christ: Preparing Adults for Baptism and Discipleship. Video. Chicago: ELCA Division for Congregational Ministries, 1998. This 18-minute video provides visual images from actual candidates in specific congregations.

Welcome to Christ: Sponsor's Guide. Minneapolis: Augsburg Fortress, 2000. This booklet provides sponsors with guidelines and resources.

What Do You Seek? Welcoming the Adult Inquirer. Minneapolis: Augsburg Fortress, 2000. This book provides guidance for the formation of baptized persons who were never catechized after their baptisms as infants.

Historical Background

Johnson, Maxwell E. *The Rites of Christian Initiation: Their Evolution and Interpretation.* Revised and expanded edition. Collegeville, Minnesota: Pueblo, 2007. The most comprehensive history available of the rites of Christian initiation from the New Testament through developments in the early twenty-first century.

Turner, Paul. *Hallelujah Highway: A History of the Catechumenate.* Chicago: Liturgy Training Publications, 2000. A thorough, accessible history of the catechumenate showing the flexibility of catechesis in various times and places.

Whitaker, E. C. *Documents of the Baptismal Liturgy.* Revised and expanded edition by Maxwell E. Johnson. Collegeville, Minnesota: Pueblo, 2003. The best collection of primary source material on how early centuries of the church prepared for and celebrated baptism.

Yarnold, Edward, SJ. *The Awe-Inspiring Rites of Initiation.* Collegeville, Minnesota: The Liturgical Press, 1994. Excerpts from the catechetical lectures/sermons of fourth-century catechists provide fascinating insights into the preparation of candidates for baptism. Yarnold also shows how the modern process in the Roman Catholic Church called the Rite of Christian Initiation of Adults (RCIA) adapts that early church process. Other denominations have also adapted that process in their own unique ways.

CONTENTS OF COMPANION CD-ROM ◉

Snapshots of Stages
Snapshot of Inquiry
Snapshot of Exploration
Snapshot of Intense Preparation
Snapshot of Baptismal Living

Basic Handouts for Participants
An Overview of the Disciple Making Process
More than Membership
Belonging
Letter to the Inquirer
My Life Story
My Story
Introduction to Exploration for People Considering Baptism
Introduction to Intense Preparation for People Enrolled for Baptism
The Three Days: A Brief Overview
Introduction to Baptismal Living for the Newly Baptized
What Is Offered to People Who Are Already Baptized?
An Overview of Rites of Discipleship
Water Life: A Bible Study on Baptism and Water Images

Useful Items for Sponsors
Guide for Sponsors
Top Ten Ideas for Sponsors

Useful Items for Disciple Making Groups
Prayers for the Faith Journey
Exercises in Identifying Ministries in Daily Life
Small Group Blessings and Prayers
Scripture Reflection Methods
Disciple Making Year Round
Baptism: Youth and Emerging Adults
Launch Guide for Making Disciples
Praying for Those Preparing for Baptism and the Newly Baptized

Denominational Disciple Making Rites

Presentation Documents
    Enrollment Book
    Apostles' Creed
    Lord's Prayer

Clip Art

*When a resource mentioned in this handbook is available on the companion CD-ROM, a ❸ symbol indicates this.